Extraordinary Popular Delusions and the Madness of Crowds

and

Confusión de Confusiones

Wiley Investment Classics

Reminiscences of a Stock Operator (1923)
    Edwin Lefevre

Where Are the Customers' Yachts or *A Good Hard Look at Wall Street* (1940)
    Fred Schwed, Jr.

The Battle for Investment Survival (1935)
    Gerald M. Loeb

Extraordinary Popular Delusions and the Madness of Crowds by Charles Mackay (1841) and *Confusión de Confusiones* by Joseph de la Vega (1688)
    Martin S. Fridson, Editor

Extraordinary
Popular Delusions and
the Madness of Crowds

and

Confusión de Confusiones

Martin S. Fridson, Editor

John Wiley & Sons, Inc.

New York • Chichester • Brisbane • Toronto • Singapore

Extraordinary Popular Delusions and the Madness of Crowds by Charles Mackay was originally published in 1841 under the title *Memoirs of Extraordinary Popular Delusions*. The present edition includes only the chapters dealing directly with speculation and financial markets.

Confusión de Confusiones has been reprinted in cooperation with Harvard University. The original manuscript is part of the Kress Library of Business and Economics at the Harvard Graduate School of Business Administration. Portions descriptive of the Amsterdam Stock Exchange selected and translated by Professor Hermann Kellenbenz.

This text is printed on acid-free paper.

Copyright © 1996 by Marketplace Books
Published by John Wiley & Sons, Inc.

ISBN   0-471-13309-4   (Cloth)

ISBN   0-471-13312-4   (Paper)

Printed in the United States of America

10   9   8   7   6   5

CONTENTS

FOREWORD

Peter L. Bernstein

The tales told in this volume cover events that happened about three hundred years ago, but the accounts sound like only yesterday, or maybe even today. That explains why these two books have held the attention of investors for so long—the more things change, the more they seem to stay the same. Nothing in our modern markets appear to make much difference, not the dazzling technology, not the institutional dominance, not the complexity of financial instruments, not the information overload, not the globalization, not the powerful insights of financial theory.

Apparently, most features of market behavior today are little different from market behavior in the seventeenth century. Speculators still speculate, while the risk-averse still hedge. But it is not just the conduct of investors that is so strikingly similar to what we see today. Even the instruments traded and the mechanics of settlement have barely changed with the passage of time.

That gives rise to an interesting question. Are our contemporary markets less sophisticated than we like to think they are? Or were those earlier markets more sophisticated than we have been led to believe? I leave the answer to the reader.

The less visible drama here emerges from the unique character of these few hundred years in the long history of humanity. The events related by Mackay and de la Vega could not possibly have occurred four hundred years ago, because there was no need for financial markets as recently as four hundred years ago. They would have made no sense at all to Henry VIII,

Pope Julius II, or the Emperor Charles V, all titans of the 1500s. The astonishing feature of both books is that markets still in their historical infancy could display behavior that is so familiar to contemporary readers.

For most of recorded history up to the seventeenth century, the total supply of wealth grew very slowly indeed. Ownership of wealth occasionally changed hands, but mostly as a result of force or death, not financial transactions. It was only after Columbus launched a veritable fever of overseas explorations in the sixteenth century that new wealth began to flow toward Europe—the produce of new lands, new supplies of raw materials, new sources of animals, to say nothing of gold and silver in formidable quantities. In the wake of all that came an avalanche of technological development that ultimately led to the industrial revolution.

Now one family or even one nation could grow richer without making some other family or nation poorer in the process— an economic and social transformation of the most fundamental character. For the very first time, the accumulation of wealth ceased to depend upon inheritance or plunder—or, at least, the plunder took place in lands far from European shores. As the total pool of wealth increased, enterprise became the driving force of ownership. The beginning of the end of the nobility dates from this moment. Note that the year in which *Confusión de Confusiones* appears, 1688, was the same year that the English threw out the Stuarts and took the first steps in the establishment of a constitutional monarchy. This dramatic break with the past is the true beginning of the modern era.

Enterprise requires capital—that is, enterprise must be financed—often in amounts greater than any one entrepreneur can gather alone. Markets for financial claims on tangible assets answer this need. The rapidity with which these markets developed, and the ready supply of liquid wealth that poured into these markets, is eloquent testimony to the pace at which Europeans were getting rich in the course of the seventeenth century.

Once financial claims come into existence, they seem to lose no time before they begin to lead lives of their own, quite detached from the underlying assets to which they owe their birth. That is the moral of the stories that Mackay and de la Vega have to tell us, so early in the financial market game. That these stories seem so much like other stories in the history of financial markets proves the durability of the moral involved. What impresses me is the rapidity with which this feature made its appearance.

I must also emphasize to the reader that this volume contains three jewels, not just two. Martin Fridson's introduction is not merely an appendage to Mackay and de la Vega: it is an integral part of the many delights that lie ahead of you as you read this remarkable history of wealth, cupidity, chicanery, and financial innovation in days gone by.

INTRODUCTION:
IN THE REALM OF THE SENSELESS

When an editor of the *Financial Times* recently chose the ten best investment books ever written, the first two titles on his list were Joseph de la Vega's *Confusión de Confusiones* and Charles Mackay's *Extraordinary Popular Delusions and the Madness of Crowds.*

The editor's decision to arrange his selections chronologically gave a decided edge to de la Vega (1688) and Mackay (1841). Even without such advantages, though, these two venerable works are fixtures on short lists of the most valuable books on the securities markets. One or both invariably show up in articles with titles such as "A Reading List for Investors," "The Library Every Investor Needs," and "Gifts That Make Financial Sense."

Investors continue to cherish de la Vega's confusions and Mackay's delusions because the market never ceases to befuddle and beguile. Onlookers reacted with bewilderment to the Dow Jones Industrial Average's 508-point plunge on October 19, 1987, much as their ancestors did when the South-Sea Bubble burst in 1720. Similarly, investors cannot fathom how Japan's Nikkei 225 could have been valued 91% higher at the beginning of 1990 than it was just nine months later.

Charles Mackay attributes such outlandish volatility to periodic outbreaks of mass hysteria. In contrast, Joseph de la

1

Vega sees cunning behind the market's convulsions. He depicts price fluctuations as the handiwork of scheming speculators.

Both explanations are worth examining if you aspire to an understanding of the stock exchange's frequently erratic behavior. From the classics of Mackay and de la Vega, *Delusions* and *Confusións* extract investment wisdom that has been judged invaluable by many of the market's greatest authorities.

For example, *Extraordinary Popular Delusions and the Madness of Crowds* was the favorite book of Bernard Baruch. Much of its present reputation is traceable to the celebrated financier. Baruch encouraged the republication of the book in 1932 and contributed an introduction. John Templeton, one of today's most successful investors, likewise holds Mackay's opus in high esteem.

If you follow the financial press avidly, you cannot avoid the praise routinely accorded *Extraordinary Popular Delusions.* In the pages of *Forbes,* various columnists have called it "the most important single book related to [the investment] business," a work "that should be in the library of every investor," "required reading for all who invest in the securities markets," and a treatise that "smart financiers often cite as their favorite text." Typical descriptions found in other publications include "the celebrated tome of economic folly," recommended reading for "all those who think 'this time is different,'" and "a book you'll wish you'd read before the stock market belly flopped in October [1987]." Another commentator simply observes, "If one works on Wall Street for any length of time, ultimately he or she is directed to the book, *Extraordinary Popular Delusions and the Madness of Crowds.*"

A century-and-a-half after first being published, Mackay's account of speculative bubbles is automatically cited in connection with every new boom or bust. Among the topics of recent years that have prompted experts to invoke *Extraordinary Popular Delusions* are gold, Mexican stocks, food company shares, housing costs, Japanese land prices, junk bonds, and the collapse of Baring Securities.

Mackay's influence extends far beyond the confines of the financial markets. A survey of the media yields allusions to

Extraordinary Popular Delusions and the Madness of Crowds in connection with computer virus protection, the confirmation hearings of Supreme Court Justice Clarence Thomas, Halley's comet, the proliferation of casino gambling, Teenage Mutant Ninja Turtles, and the Power Rangers. Commentators draw parallels between the episodes recounted by Mackay and such diverse occurrences as the improbable box office success of atrocious movies, campaigns to reduce violence, debates over damage to the ozone, a poisoned fruit scare, fears of abuse at child care centers, and efforts to upgrade sewage treatment. A 1992 book was entitled *Ponzi Schemes, Invaders from Mars & More Extraordinary Popular Delusions and the Madness of Crowds.* Perhaps the ultimate cultural homage to Mackay was an art exhibition of the same year, *Popular Delusions and the Madness of Crowds,* which explored "what happens when individuals cease to take responsibility for themselves."

It is not overstating the matter to say that Mackay's book has by now passed into legend. In the retelling, the story has been magnified, embellished, and, inevitably, garbled. Some sources correctly indicate that *Extraordinary Popular Delusions and the Madness of Crowds* first appeared in 1841, while others say 1852, the year of the second edition. A 1991 article establishes *Extraordinary Popular Delusions* as a cult classic, describing it as out-of-print since 1956. Other writers, however, mention editions in 1974, 1976, 1980, and 1985. (*Books in Print* currently lists publication dates of 1980, 1986, and 1991.) Compounding the confusion is the change of titles between Mackay's first and second editions, from *Memoirs of Extraordinary Popular Delusions* to *Memoirs of Extraordinary Popular Delusions and the Madness of Crowds.* "Memoirs" was dropped in the 1932 edition.

In 1929, by most accounts, Bernard Baruch preserved his immense wealth by heeding Mackay's lessons. One periodical says, on the contrary, that Baruch ignored the sound advice he gave others and plunged back into the market before the crash. The truth is that Baruch emerged from the debacle with his fortune largely intact. According to a biographer, though, he found that being a prophet of doom was causing people to ignore his opinion. In response, Baruch switched to a more bullish line in his public pronouncements. A dual legend has consequently arisen. On the one hand, admirers say that Baruch foresaw the 1929 crash, partly by remembering the antecedents described in *Extraordinary Popular Delusions*. Liberal historians, in contrast, cite Baruch's optimistic comments as evidence of precisely the sort of market mania that Mackay decried.

Sources variously describe the author of *Extraordinary Popular Delusions* as a nineteenth century barrister, an English chronicler, and a Scottish journalist. In reality, the Scottish-born Mackay appended "LL.D." to his name after being awarded that degree by Glasgow University, but never practiced law. His renown as a poet and songwriter was at least as great as his journalistic reputation. So fleeting is fame, however, that one citation gives his name as Bernard Mackay.

No run-of-the-mill investment book could inspire such a steady flow of misinformation. *Extraordinary Popular Delusions* is clearly in a special class, as indicated by the many investment managers who tell interviewers that they keep it forever close at hand. Not so obvious is the reason for the book's enduring popularity. After all, Mackay lays out no trading rules or formulas for valuing securities. It's curious that a work invariably found on investors' reading lists is so unlike the typical investment manual.

Certainly, the incidents that Mackay describes have intrinsic interest. Readers are bound to be amused by his colorful depictions of the Dutch tulip bulb craze, the Mississippi Scheme, and the South-Sea Bubble. But there's considerably more to the story than pure entertainment. Mackay's theme appeals to everyone who hopes to prosper by proving the majority in error. This is a group to which all speculators belong, along with purveyors of opinions on a wide array of nonfinancial issues. In Mackay's book, they find affirmation that the consensus is fallible.

The message of *Extraordinary Popular Delusions* goes beyond the mere notion that people en masse sometimes behave irrationally. By Mackay's account, the crowd's hysteria is easily detectable by individuals who rely on common sense. Immense profits are to be had if this assertion is correct and Mackay has little doubt that it is. He portrays collective misjudgments so gross that seemingly only a dullard could fail to perceive them.

To be sure, life was much simpler for financial commentators in the middle of the nineteenth century. Mathematician Louis Bachelier hadn't yet calculated that stock prices moved in a patternless "random walk." This conclusion cast serious doubt on the feasibility of divining the market's future course, even when it appeared to have overshot in one direction or the other. Furthermore, it was only long after Mackay's death that economists began to question the reality of speculative bubbles. New theories suggested that even apparently absurd price swings could reflect bona fide changes in asset values. Later, in reaction to such thinking, a school of Inefficient Markets theorists reasserted the importance of fads and follies. By then, arcane mathematical methods had overshadowed attempts to dissect the mind of the market.

This is not to say that Mackay's specialty of historical narrative has lost its place in the discussion. Since his time, however, the level of debate has escalated. Analysts have developed a troublesome habit of checking the facts behind published accounts, rather than accepting them as authoritative sources for citation. In the course of this change, the nineteenth century's more casual approach to research hasn't stood Mackay in good stead.

Analysis by Peter M. Garber of Brown University shows that Mackay sloppily assembled his history of the tulip bulb craze from secondhand sources. Abraham Munting's "folio volume of one thousand pages upon the tulipomania" was in reality a botanical treatise with no more than six pages touching on the affair. Furthermore, Garber flatly accuses Mackay of plagiarizing a late eighteenth-century account by one Johann Beckmann, adding that Mackay's version was in turn plagiarized by P.T. Barnum. Still more damaging is Garber's blast at the favorite anecdote of countless readers of *Extraordinary Popular Delusions.* His research suggests that the sailor who ate an extremely precious bulb, thinking it was an onion, probably enjoyed his costly meal at some point later than the 1634–1637 speculation.

Such quibbles are not the real point of Garber's critique. Rather, he attacks the very notion that there was an irrational explosion in tulip prices during the years chronicled by Mackay. Through meticulous study of market movements, Garber shows that comparably large price swings in rare varieties of bulbs occurred in both earlier and later periods. Unrestrained speculation evidently affected only the more common varieties, which were traded in informal futures markets established in taverns during the winter of 1636–1637.

Granting all of Garber's points, isn't it nevertheless obvious that things got overdone if a single *Semper Augustus* bulb sold for the equivalent of $50,000? Not really. Garber points to a recent sale of a small quantity of lily bulbs for $500,000. An especially beautiful tulip bulb has a unique ability to produce descendants with its distinctive coloration and pattern. Frederic S. Mishkin of Columbia University notes that in time, millions of such descendants may exist:

> The net result is that even though one hundred years down the road the price of an individual descended from the original bulb is only a tiny fraction of the initial bulb price, the high price of the original bulb is completely sensible. The reason is that the present value of all the millions of descendant bulbs produced from the original bulb can be an extremely high figure indeed.

Just as Garber demythologizes tulipomania, Larry D. Neal of the University of Illinois-Urbana challenges the traditional interpretation of the South Sea Bubble as "simply a wild mania or as a massive swindle." In his estimation, the South Sea Company initially served a useful purpose by converting government war debts into liquid, low-interest securities. The company erred, says Neal, only by overreaching and promising more than it could deliver.

No amount of scholarly debunking, however, is likely to extinguish the fondness of investors for *Extraordinary Popular Delusions*. As long as people stake money on their ability to outsmart the majority opinion, they'll cherish the thought that the majority periodically becomes deranged. Speculators will always agree with Kipling that, "If you can keep your head when all about you are losing theirs, [then] yours is the Earth and everything that's in it."

Whether or not it conforms to all of today's economic theories and standards of scholarship, *Extraordinary Popular Delusions and the Madness of Crowds* has a secure place on investors' recommended reading lists. The book cuts to the heart of an eternal query: Are there clear, unmistakable signs that it's time to buy or to sell?

Mackay's narrative makes a forceful case that when a price trend is overdone, fine-tuned analysis becomes superfluous. Nevertheless, "obviously" overvalued markets sometimes proceed to become even more overvalued. It's not a bad idea, therefore, to leaven Mackay's emphasis on mass hysteria with Joseph de la Vega's attention to the coldly calculating side of things.

The author of *Confusión de Confusiones* sets his sights narrowly. He focuses on his own era and on the traffic in a single security, the stock of the Dutch East India Company. Furthermore, de la Vega writes from the idiosyncratic perspective of a poet-businessman, raised in Amsterdam in a community of refugees from the Spanish Inquisition. Three centuries later, however, *Confusión de Confusiones* exudes universality as it describes trading gambits that have never gone out of fashion.

As an example, de la Vega distinguishes three varieties of stock market participants that are observable in our own time. Certain investors merely collect dividends and "do not care about movements in the price of the stock." Others pursue conservative trading strategies based on short-term economic and political forecasts. A third group consists of outright speculators.

De la Vega also differentiates fundamental analysis from the technical variety, which he labels "opinion on the stock exchange itself." He enunciates the present-day principle of buying on the rumor and selling on the news. ("The expectation of an event creates a much deeper impression upon the exchange than the event itself.") In modern parlance, the "Greater Fool Theory" describes de la Vega's notion that the investor need not be alarmed by excessively high prices. ("Be aware of the fact that there are as many speculators as there are people, and that there will always be buyers who will free you from anxiety . . .") The contemporary phrase "smart money" aptly describes the cunning speculators who, according to de la Vega, attract "untold hosts of adherents."

Reading *Confusión de Confusiones* leaves a distinct impression that any innovation in the trading of securities during the last three hundred years has been of an incidental nature. Less than a century after the stock market's origin, forward sales and option trading were well-established practices. For odd-lotters, there were phantom "ducaton shares," each with a nominal value one-tenth that of a real share.

Securities regulators, too, were already on the scene in de la Vega's day. In fact, they had devised a means of discouraging market manipulation that is no longer in use. The market watchdogs outlawed short sales, but didn't bother to enforce the rule. Instead, they allowed the losers in such transactions to renege through an "appeal to Frederick."

The possibility of having one's profits snatched away would seem to be an effective deterrent to scofflaws. Then as now, however, market regulation couldn't entirely squelch the freebooting tendencies of stock speculators. Traders defied efforts to control their activities by forming rings and carrying out a dizzying array of manipulative ruses. According to de la Vega, the bears spread rumors, foiled the bulls by locking up all available margin capital, and created fear of a war or political crisis by driving down government bond prices. Bulls, for their part, disseminated fictitious quotations, fabricated buy orders, and ensnared the bears by pretending to join their ranks.

So elaborate are the intrigues catalogued by de la Vega that he might have entitled his treatise *Collusion of Collusions.* As he portrays it, the confusion of investors isn't primarily a matter of manias or delusions. Instead, the market's gyrations reflect carefully orchestrated schemes to move prices without regard to fundamental considerations. Because these plots do not depend on genuine news to precipitate rallies or selloffs, the resulting changes in direction are inexplicable to anybody outside the conspiracy.

Today, just as in de la Vega's time, bewildered investors struggle to make sense out of apparent chaos. Mystified by the disparity between prices and fundamental values, they search for patterns in the prices themselves. Perhaps, they surmise, if the market goes down for so many days in a row, it must then go up. Alternatively, there may be significance in a rise in the rate at which prices are rising.

Wall Street wisdom—such as it is—largely revolves around these eternal quandaries. And because the questions are never settled in one direction or the other, investment pundits thrive by dispensing conspicuously contradictory maxims. According to one popular rule, investors should cut their losses and allow their profits to run. On the other hand, warn the sage veterans, "The greedy become the needy." Another chestnut goes, "There are bulls, there are bears, and there are pigs." So which is it? Should investors resist the urge to cash in while they're ahead or should they take the money and run?

For the record, de la Vega comes down on the side of the bird in the hand. ("Take every gain without showing remorse about missed profits. . . .") Certain market gurus, however, claim that knowing which way to go at any particular juncture is the easy part. All that's required is one of those infallible trading systems, which the market technicians can easily supply. The real reason that everyone isn't getting rich, according to this school of thought, is psychological. People deviate from their trading disciplines because they surrender to emotion, probably as the result of some childhood trauma.

Fortunately, the malady has a cure. At least, it has if we are to believe a special breed of consultants who gladly offer the remedy for a fee. These experts claim that investors can overcome their irrational impulses through psychological counseling.

Naturally, the treatment comes with no guarantee of profitable trading results. In fact, the clinical evidence supporting investor therapy is thin. For example, if *mens sana* is essential to profitable trading, how can we explain the apparent success of John Mulheren, the head of Buffalo Partners? Not only does Mulheren freely acknowledge that he suffers from manic depression, but he has celebrated the fact by opening an ice cream parlor called Crazee's.

Confusión de Confusiones doesn't neglect the stock market's psychological dimension. On the other hand, de la Vega never suggests that profitable trading is a mere matter of overcoming mental blocks. After all, there's no benefit in being clear-headed if the source of market fluctuations is beyond the realm of the senses. De la Vega is less in tune with the self-help crowd than with those who credit the all-powerful *They* with every twist and turn in securities prices.

The image of a market dominated by cabals is as popular as ever, notwithstanding contemporary prohibitions on manipulation and insider trading. Many investors believe implicitly that if prices are falling for no obvious reason, it's because *They* are "taking 'em down." Whenever a stock is breaking out on the upside, with no news on the tape to explain it, *They* know something that others don't. Perhaps there's a touch of paranoia involved, but investors find comfort in the belief that their losses are invariably the product of some dastardly plot. Periodic revelations of illegal trading practices more than suffice to sustain the story's plausibility.

De la Vega's emphasis on conspiracies strikes a sympathetic chord with a sizable segment of investors. On close reading, though, *Confusión de Confusiones* presents a more complex and credible picture than a market totally at the mercy of omnipotent colluders. De la Vega portrays the bears perpetually contending with the bulls. Consequently, neither party can consistently move stock prices at will. Abrupt changes in economic fundamentals, which generally are not foreseen, periodically give one side or the other the upper hand.

Consider de la Vega's analysis of the crash of 1688. In his view, the calm that preceded the debacle reflected a combination of plentiful credit, international security, favorable trade prospects, and good demographics, culminating in an upbeat business outlook. Positive news then arrived in the form of expanded trade opportunities and the discovery of new ore bodies. Amidst the prevailing optimism, no one heeded reports of a possible negative earnings surprise. According to de la Vega, investors factored into their calculations miraculous economic performance, which was widely expected yet bound "to surprise everybody." (Simple logic exposes such an event as a contradiction in terms, albeit one that troubles market commentators no more today than it did three hundred years ago.) Even the majority of the bears capitulated to the bullish sentiment. Because they were unwilling to sell short, the market lacked technical support when reports of an earnings shortfall precipitated massive selling and margin calls.

Up to this point in de la Vega's narrative, there's little cause for confusion. The market initially rose on the basis of the best available information, which was interpreted correctly. Perhaps investors' expectations became excessive at some point, although it's impossible to judge from the limited data that the author provides. At any rate, the unfavorable news could not have been foreseen. Had the bears muttered, "Tsk, tsk, this is another example of irrational overshooting" and sold short, they easily might have lost their shirts. In the event, the bears suffered a calamity by turning bullish. Far from being omnipotent, *They* were powerless to move the market at will, for all their scheming. Nor did volatility alone demonstrate irrationality on the part of investors. By de la Vega's account, shifting fundamentals justified a revision in prices.

The denouement of the crash of 1688 is less reassuring to those who conceive of rational markets and a fair game. Despite the initial assessment, the Dutch East India Company's profits turned out to be excellent. But instead of rallying, the market fell on false rumors of war and a tax hike to fund an increased defense budget. According to de la Vega, the bears managed to stampede even those who rightly suspected that the talk of war was unfounded. Anyone viewing the Amsterdam exchange with Efficient Market blinders, but without being in on the bears' scheme, would have been totally confused. Had Charles Mackay been present, he would have felt vindicated in his judgment that investors "go mad in herds [and] recover their senses slowly."

Human nature seemingly has changed little since the initial publication of *Confusión de Confusiones* and the appearance of *Extraordinary Popular Delusions and the Madness of Crowds* a hundred and fifty years later. The current emergence of new securities markets around the globe is teaching the old lessons all over again. Giddy enthusiasm for Latin American issues during 1993 was replaced by temporary revulsion when Mexico abruptly devalued its currency late in 1994. Plainly, extreme swings in investor sentiment are as much a feature of today's market as they were in the time of John Law and the Mississippi Scheme. In fact, Russia's volatile young stock market has already produced a worthy successor to Law.

Sergei Mavrodi reportedly became his country's fifth richest man by guaranteeing investors an annual return of 3,000%. His vehicle was a mysterious investment fund called MMM. The shares of MMM were not traded on any exchange, but rather bought and sold by the fund at prices established by Mavrodi. Within six months of the initial offering, the enterprising ex-mathematician had boosted MMM stock from $1 to $60. Skeptics concluded, in the absence of evidence that the fund held any tangible assets, that MMM must be a Ponzi scheme. That is, they surmised that Mavrodi was paying off early investors with funds taken in at higher prices from later buyers. When he was no longer able to continue buying back shares, the price plummeted to 46 cents, a 99% decline from the peak.

Luckily for Mavrodi, Russia had no law against Ponzi schemes. Prosecutors threatened him with charges of tax evasion, but at least initially, they met with no greater success than they had in their similar attempts to convict him in 1992–1993. Mavrodi announced his candidacy for a parliamentary seat that had become vacant when the incumbent was gunned down, gangland-style. Upon winning the election, Mavrodi claimed immunity from prosecution.

Remarkably, investors seemed to bear Mavrodi little malice. "I knew it was a pyramid scheme," said one young widow, as she stood in line in the rain to purchase MMM shares *after* the price collapse. The stock was cheap, she reckoned, and might skyrocket once again. A stockbroker who had gotten out just before the panic began, clearing a $50,000 profit, was downright philosophical about the affair. "Of course Mavrodi deceived many people," he conceded, "but there's no free lunch." (Economist Milton Friedman probably had something very different in mind when he popularized that phrase, notwithstanding his strong advocacy of unfettered markets.) On the whole, Russians appeared to blame MMM's downfall less on its president than on government officials who had bad-mouthed the venture.

Investors' boundless faith in Mavrodi confirms the timelessness of de la Vega's confusions and Mackay's delusions. Perhaps it's true that advances in theory enable present-day economists to perceive greater rationality in market perturbations than their predecessors could. But the theorists must somehow account for the investors who clamored to buy a new MMM offering, even after losing nearly their entire investments in a scheme they acknowledged to be nothing but a glorified chain letter. The persistence of such folly sustains the hope that a truly rational investor can capitalize on the crowd's madness.

Accordingly, the episodes recounted in *Confusións* and *Delusions* will surely grace investors' recommended reading lists for many years to come. The Bernard Baruchs of the twenty-first century will undoubtedly confide to interviewers that they consult these texts religiously. And today's rookie traders will pass on the works of de la Vega and Mackay to their successors, not because they're ancient, but because their message remains as compelling as ever.

Extraordinary
Popular Delusions and
the Madness of Crowds

———•◆•———

Charles Mackay
1841

PREFACE

The object of the Author in the following pages has been to collect the most remarkable instances of those moral epidemics which have been excited, sometimes by one cause and sometimes by another, and to show how easily the masses have been led astray, and how imitative and gregarious men are, even in their infatuations and crimes.

Some of the subjects introduced may be familiar to the reader; but the Author hopes that sufficient novelty of detail will be found even in these, to render them acceptable, while they could not be wholly omitted in justice to the subject of which it was proposed to treat. The memoirs of the South Sea madness and the Mississippi delusion are more complete and copious than are to be found elsewhere; and the same may be said of the history of the Witch Mania,* which contains an account of its terrific progress in Germany, a part of the subject which has been left comparatively untouched by Sir Walter Scott, in his "Letters on Demonology and Witchcraft," the most important that have yet appeared on this fearful but most interesting subject.

Popular delusions began so early, spread so widely, and have lasted so long, that instead of two or three volumes, fifty would scarcely suffice to detail their history. The present may be considered more of a miscellany of delusions than a history,—a chapter only in the great and awful book of human folly which yet remains to be written, and which Porson once jestingly said he would write in five hundred volumes! Interspersed are sketches of some lighter matters,—amusing instances of the imitativeness and wrongheadedness of the people, rather than examples of folly and delusion.

Editor's Note: The reference to Witch Mania on this page and Alchemy on page 18 relate to chapters in Mackay's book that are not included in this reprint. This reprint contains only those chapters that directly relate to speculation and financial markets.

Religious manias have been purposely excluded as incompatible with the limits prescribed to the present work;—a mere list of them would alone be sufficient to occupy a volume.

In another volume should these be favourably received, the Author will attempt a complete view of the progress of Alchemy and the philosophical delusions that sprang from it, including the Rosicrucians of a bygone, and the Magnetisers of the present, era.

London, April 23rd, 1841.

CONTENTS

with the scheme examined—Their respective punishments—Concluding remarks.

THE TULIPOMANIA

Conrad Gesner—Tulips brought from Vienna to England—Rage for the tulip among the Dutch—Its great value—Curious anecdote of a sailor and a tulip—Regular marts for tulips—Tulips employed as a means of speculation—Great depreciation in their value—End of the mania.

MONEY MANIA.—
THE MISSISSIPPI SCHEME

Some in clandestine companies combine;
Erect new stocks to trade beyond the line;
With air and empty names beguile the town,
And raise new credits first, then cry 'em down;
Divide the empty nothing into shares,
And set the crowd together by the ears.—*Defoe.*

The personal character and career of one man are so intimately connected with the great scheme of the years 1719 and 1720, that a history of the Mississippi madness can have no fitter introduction than a sketch of the life of its great author John Law. Historians are divided in opinion as to whether they should designate him a knave or a madman. Both epithets were unsparingly applied to him in his lifetime, and while the unhappy consequences of his projects were still deeply felt. Posterity, however, has found reason to doubt the justice of the accusation, and to confess that John Law was neither knave nor madman, but one more deceived than deceiving, more sinned against than sinning. He was thoroughly acquainted with the philosophy and true principles of credit. He understood the monetary question better than any man of his day; and if his system fell with a crash so tremendous, it was not so much his fault as that of the people amongst whom he had erected it. He did not calculate upon the avaricious frenzy of a whole nation; he did not see that confidence, like mistrust, could be increased almost *ad infinitum,* and that hope was as extravagant as fear. How was he to foretell that the French people, like the man in the fable, would kill, in their frantic eagerness, the fine goose he had brought to lay them so many golden eggs? His fate

was like that which may be supposed to have overtaken the first adventurous boatman who rowed from Erie to Ontario. Broad and smooth was the river on which he embarked; rapid and pleasant was his progress; and who was to stay him in his career? Alas for him! the cataract was nigh. He saw, when it was too late, that the tide which wafted him so joyously along was a tide of destruction; and when he endeavoured to retrace his way, he found that the current was too strong for his weak efforts to stem, and that he drew nearer every instant to the tremendous falls. Down he went over the sharp rocks, and the waters with him. *He* was dashed to pieces with his bark; but the waters, maddened and turned to foam by the rough descent, only boiled and bubbled for a time, and then flowed on again as smoothly as ever. Just so it was with Law and the French people. He was the boatman, and they were the waters.

John Law was born at Edinburgh in the year 1671. His father was the younger son of an ancient family in Fife, and carried on the business of a goldsmith and banker. He amassed considerable wealth in his trade, sufficient to enable him to gratify the wish, so common among his countrymen, of adding a territorial designation to his name. He purchased with this view the estates of Lauriston and Randleston, on the Firth of Forth, on the borders of West and Mid Lothian, and was thenceforth known as Law of Lauriston. The subject of our memoir, being the eldest son, was received into his father's counting-house at the age of fourteen, and for three years laboured hard to acquire an insight into the principles of banking as then carried on in Scotland. He had always manifested great love for the study of numbers, and his proficiency in the mathematics was considered extraordinary in one of his tender years. At the age of seventeen he was tall, strong, and well made; and his face, although deeply scarred with the small-pox, was agreeable in its expression, and full of intelligence. At this time he began to neglect his business, and becoming vain of his person, indulged in considerable extravagance of attire. He was a great favourite with the ladies, by whom he was called Beau Law; while the other sex, despising his foppery, nicknamed him Jessamy John. At the death of his father, which happened in 1688, he withdrew entirely from the desk, which had become so irksome, and being possessed of the revenues of the paternal estate of Lauriston, he proceeded to London, to see the world.

He was now very young, very vain, good-looking, tolerably rich, and quite uncontrolled. It is no wonder that, on his arrival in the capital, he should launch out into extravagance. He soon became a regular frequenter of the gaming-houses, and by pursuing a certain plan, based upon some abstruse calculation of chances, he contrived to gain considerable sums. All the gamblers envied him his luck, and many made it a point to watch his play, and stake their money on the same chances. In affairs of gallantry he was equally fortunate; ladies of the first rank smiled graciously upon the handsome Scotchman—the young, the rich, the witty, and the obliging. But all these successes only paved the way for reverses. After he had been for nine years exposed to the dangerous attractions of the gay life he was leading, he became an irrecoverable gambler. As his love of play increased in violence, it diminished in prudence. Great losses were only to be repaired by still greater ventures, and one unhappy day he lost more than he could repay without mortgaging his family estate. To that step he was driven at last. At the same time his gallantry brought him into trouble. A love affair, or slight flirtation, with a lady of the name of Villiers,* exposed him to the resentment of a Mr. Wilson, by whom he was challenged to fight a duel. Law accepted, and had the ill fortune to shoot his antagonist dead upon the spot. He was arrested the same day, and brought to trial for murder by the relatives of Mr. Wilson. He was afterwards found guilty, and sentenced to death. The sentence was commuted to a fine, upon the ground that the offence only amounted to manslaughter. An appeal being lodged by a brother of the deceased, Law was detained in the King's Bench, whence, by some means or other, which he never explained, he contrived to escape; and

---

* Miss Elizabeth Villiers, afterwards Countess of Orkney.

an action being instituted against the sheriffs, he was advertised in the Gazette, and a reward offered for his apprehension. He was described as "Captain John Law, a Scotchman, aged twenty-six; a very tall, black, lean man; well shaped, above six feet high, with large pock-holes in his face; big nosed, and speaking broad and loud." As this was rather a caricature than a description of him, it has been supposed that it was drawn up with a view to favour his escape. He succeeded in reaching the Continent, where he travelled for three years, and devoted much of his attention to the monetary and banking affairs of the countries through which he passed. He stayed a few months in Amsterdam, and speculated to some extent in the funds. His mornings were devoted to the study of finance and the principles of trade, and his evenings to the gaming-house. It is generally believed that he returned to Edinburgh in the year 1700. It is certain that he published in that city his *Proposals and Reasons for constituting a Council of Trade.* This pamphlet did not excite much attention.

In a short time afterwards he published a project for establishing what he called a Land-Bank,* the notes issued by which were never to exceed the value of the entire lands of the state, upon ordinary interest, or were to be equal in value to the land, the right to enter into possession at a certain time. The project excited a good deal of discussion in the Scottish Parliament, and a motion for the establishment of such a bank was brought forward by a neutral party, called the Squadrone, whom Law had interested in his favour. The Parliament ultimately passed a resolution to the effect, that, to establish any kind of paper credit, so as to force it to pass, was an improper expedient for the nation.

Upon the failure of this project, and of his efforts to procure a pardon for the murder of Mr. Wilson, Law withdrew to the Continent, and resumed his old habits of gaming. For fourteen years he continued to roam about, in Flanders, Holland, Germany, Hungary, Italy, and France. He soon became

---

* The wits of the day called it a *sand-bank,* which would wreck the vessel of the state.

intimately acquainted with the extent of the trade and resources of each, and daily more confirmed in his opinion that
no country could prosper without a paper currency. During
the whole of this time he appears to have chiefly supported
himself by successful play. At every gambling-house of note in
the capitals of Europe he was known and appreciated as one
better skilled in the intricacies of chance than any other man of
the day. It is stated in the *Biographie Universelle* that he was
expelled, first from Venice, and afterwards from Genoa, by the
magistrates, who thought him a visitor too dangerous for the
youth of those cities. During his residence in Paris he rendered
himself obnoxious to D'Argenson, the lieutenant-general of the
police, by whom he was ordered to quit the capital. This did
not take place, however, before he had made the acquaintance,
in the saloons, of the Duke de Vendôme, the Prince de Conti,
and of the gay Duke of Orleans, the latter of whom was destined afterwards to exercise so much influence over his fate.
The Duke of Orleans was pleased with the vivacity and good
sense of the Scottish adventurer, while the latter was no less
pleased with the wit and amiability of a prince who promised
to become his patron. They were often thrown into each
other's society, and Law seized every opportunity to instil his
financial doctrines into the mind of one whose proximity to
the throne pointed him out as destined, at no very distant date,
to play an important part in the government.

Shortly before the death of Louis XIV., or, as some say, in
1780, Law proposed a scheme of finance to Desmarets, the
comptroller. Louis is reported to have inquired whether the
projector were a Catholic, and on being answered in the negative, to have declined having any thing to do with him.*

---

* This anecdote, which is related in the correspondence of Madame de Bavière,
Duchess of Orleans and mother of the Regent, is discredited by Lord John Russell in
his *History of the principal States of Europe from the Peace of Utrecht;* for what
reason he does not inform us. There is no doubt that Law proposed his scheme to
Desmarets, and that Louis refused to hear it. The reason given for the refusal is quite
consistent with the character of that bigoted and tyrannical monarch.

It was after this repulse that he visited Italy. His mind being still occupied with schemes of finance, he proposed to Victor Amadeus, Duke of Savoy, to establish his land-bank in that country. The duke replied that his dominions were too circumscribed for the execution of so great a project, and that he was by far too poor a potentate to be ruined. He advised him, however, to try the king of France once more; for he was sure, if he knew any thing of the French character, that the people would be delighted with a plan, not only so new, but so plausible.

Louis XIV. died in 1715, and the heir to the throne being an infant only seven years of age, the Duke of Orleans assumed the reins of government, as regent, during his minority. Law now found himself in a more favourable position. The tide in his affairs had come, which, taken at the flood, was to waft him on to fortune. The regent was his friend, already acquainted with his theory and pretensions, and inclined, moreover, to aid him in any efforts to restore the wounded credit of France, bowed down to the earth by the extravagance of the long reign of Louis XIV.

Hardly was that monarch laid in his grave ere the popular hatred, suppressed so long, burst forth against his memory. He who, during his life, had been flattered with an excess of adulation, to which history scarcely offers a parallel, was now cursed as a tyrant, a bigot, and a plunderer. His statues were pelted and disfigured; his effigies torn down, amid the execrations of the populace, and his name rendered synonymous with selfishness and oppression. The glory of his arms was forgotten, and nothing was remembered but his reverses, his extravagance, and his cruelty.

The finances of the country were in a state of the utmost disorder. A profuse and corrupt monarch, whose profuseness and corruption were imitated by almost every functionary, from the highest to the lowest grade, had brought France to the verge of ruin. The national debt amounted to 3000 millions of livres, the revenue to 145 millions, and the expenses of government to 142 millions per annum; leaving only three millions to pay the interest upon 3000 millions. The first care of the regent was to discover a remedy for an evil of such magnitude, and a council was early summoned to take the matter into consideration. The Duke de St. Simon was of opinion that nothing could save the country from revolution but a remedy at once bold and dangerous. He advised the regent to convoke the states-general, and declare a national bankruptcy. The Duke de Noailles, a man of accommodating principles, an accomplished courtier, and totally averse from giving himself any trouble or annoyance that ingenuity could escape from, opposed the project of St. Simon with all his influence. He represented the expedient as alike dishonest and ruinous. The regent was of the same opinion, and this desperate remedy fell to the ground.

The measures ultimately adopted, though they promised fair, only aggravated the evil. The first and most dishonest measure was of no advantage to the state. A recoinage was ordered, by which the currency was depreciated one-fifth; those who took a thousand pieces of gold or silver to the mint received back an amount of coin of the same nominal value, but only four-fifths of the weight of metal. By this contrivance the treasury gained seventy-two millions of livres, and all the commercial operations of the country were disordered. A trifling diminution of the taxes silenced the clamours of the people, and for the slight present advantage the great prospective evil was forgotten.

A Chamber of Justice was next instituted to inquire into the malversations of the loan-contractors and the farmers of the revenues. Tax-collectors are never very popular in any country, but those of France at this period deserved all the odium with which they were loaded. As soon as these farmers-general, with all their hosts of subordinate agents, called *maltôtiers,** were called to account for their misdeeds, the most extravagant joy took possession of the nation. The Chamber of Justice, instituted chiefly for this purpose, was endowed with very extensive powers. It was composed of the presidents and councils of the parliament, the judges of the Courts of Aid and of Requests, and the

---

.* From *maltôte*, an oppressive tax.

officers of the Chamber of Account, under the general presidence of the minister of finance. Informers were encouraged to give evidence against the offenders by the promise of one-fifth part of the fines and confiscations. A tenth of all concealed effects belonging to the guilty was promised to such as should furnish the means of discovering them.

The promulgation of the edict constituting this court caused a degree of consternation among those principally concerned, which can only be accounted for on the supposition that their peculation had been enormous. But they met with no sympathy. The proceedings against them justified their terror. The Bastille was soon unable to contain the prisoners that were sent to it, and the gaols all over the country teemed with guilty or suspected persons. An order was issued to all innkeepers and postmasters to refuse horses to such as endeavoured to seek safety in flight; and all persons were forbidden, under heavy fines, to harbour them or favour their evasion. Some were condemned to the pillory, others to the galleys, and the least guilty to fine and imprisonment. One only, Samuel Bernard, a rich banker and farmer-general of a province remote from the capital, was sentenced to death. So great had been the illegal profits of this man,—looked upon as the tyrant and oppressor of his district,—that he offered six millions of livres, or 250,000*l.* sterling, to be allowed to escape.

His bribe was refused, and he suffered the penalty of death. Others, perhaps more guilty, were more fortunate. Confiscation, owing to the concealment of their treasures by the delinquents, often produced less money than a fine. The severity of the government relaxed, and fines, under the denomination of taxes, were indiscriminately levied upon all offenders; but so corrupt was every department of the administration, that the country benefited but little by the sums which thus flowed into the treasury. Courtiers and courtiers' wives and mistresses came in for the chief share of the spoils. One contractor had been taxed, in proportion to his wealth and guilt, the sum of twelve millions of livres. The Count * * *, a man of some weight in the government, called upon him, and offered to procure a remission of the fine if he would give him a hundred thousand crowns. "Vous êtes trop tard, mon ami;" replied the financier; "I have already made a bargain with your wife for fifty thousand."*

About a hundred and eighty millions of livres were levied in this manner, of which eighty were applied in payment of the debts contracted by the government. The remainder found its way into the pockets of the courtiers. Madame de Maintenon, writing on this subject, says—"We hear every day of some new grant of the regent. The people murmur very much at this mode of employing the money taken from the peculators." The people, who, after the first burst of their resentment is over, generally express a sympathy for the weak, were indignant that so much severity should be used to so little purpose. They did not see the justice of robbing one set of rogues to fatten another. In a few months all the more guilty had been brought to punishment, and the Chamber of Justice looked for victims in humbler walks of life. Charges of fraud and extortion were brought against tradesmen of good character in consequence of the great inducements held out to common informers. They were compelled to lay open their affairs before this tribunal in order to establish their innocence. The voice of complaint resounded from every side; and at the expiration of a year the government found it advisable to discontinue further proceedings. The Chamber of Justice was suppressed, and a general amnesty granted to all against whom no charges had yet been preferred.

In the midst of this financial confusion Law appeared upon the scene. No man felt more deeply than the regent the deplorable state of the country, but no man could be more averse from putting his shoulders manfully to the wheel. He

---

*This anecdote is related by M. de la Hode, in his *Life of Philippe of Orleans*. It would have looked more authentic if he had given the names of the dishonest contractor and the still more dishonest minister. But M. de la Hode's book is liable to the same objection as most of the French memoirs of that and of subsequent periods. It is sufficient with most of them that an anecdote be *ben trovato;* the *vero* is but matter of secondary consideration.

disliked business; he signed official documents without proper examination, and trusted to others what he should have undertaken himself. The cares inseparable from his high office were burdensome to him. He saw that something was necessary to be done; but he lacked the energy to do it, and had not virtue enough to sacrifice his ease and his pleasures in the attempt. No wonder that, with this character, he listened favourably to the mighty projects, so easy of execution, of the clever adventurer whom he had formerly known, and whose talents he appreciated.

When Law presented himself at court he was most cordially received. He offered two memorials to the regent, in which he set forth the evils that had befallen France, owing to an insufficient currency, at different times depreciated. He asserted that a metallic currency, unaided by a paper money, was wholly inadequate to the wants of a commercial country, and particularly cited the examples of Great Britain and Holland to shew the advantages of paper. He used many sound arguments on the subject of credit, and proposed as a means of restoring that of France, then at so low an ebb among the nations, that he should be allowed to set up a bank, which should have the management of the royal revenues, and issue notes both on that and on landed security. He further proposed that this bank should be administered in the king's name, but subject to the control of commissioners to be named by the States-General.

While these memorials were under consideration, Law translated into French his essay on money and trade, and used every means to extend through the nation his renown as a financier. He soon became talked of. The confidants of the regent spread abroad his praise, and every one expected great things of Monsieur Lass.*

On the 5th of May, 1716, a royal edict was published, by which Law was authorised, in conjunction with his brother, to

---

* The French pronounced his name in this manner to avoid the ungallic sound, *aw*. After the failure of his scheme, the wags said the nation was *lasse de lui*, and proposed that he should in future be known by the name of Monsieur He*las!*

establish a bank under the name of Law and Company, the notes of which should be received in payment of the taxes. The capital was fixed at six millions of livres, in twelve thousand shares of five hundred livres each, purchasable one fourth in specie, and the remainder in *billets d'état.* It was not thought expedient to grant him the whole of the privileges prayed for in his memorials until experience should have shewn their safety and advantage.

Law was now on the high road to fortune. The study of thirty years was brought to guide him in the management of his bank. He made all his notes payable at sight, and in the coin current at the time they were issued. This last was a master-stroke of policy, and immediately rendered his notes more valuable than the precious metals. The latter were constantly liable to depreciation by the unwise tampering of the government. A thousand livres of silver might be worth their nominal value one day, and be reduced one-sixth the next, but a note of Law's bank retained its original value. He publicly declared at the same time, that a banker deserved death if he made issues without having sufficient security to answer all demands. The consequence was, that his notes advanced rapidly in public estimation, and were received at one per cent more than specie. It was not long before the trade of the country felt the benefit. Languishing commerce began to lift up her head; the taxes were paid with greater regularity and less murmuring; and a degree of confidence was established that could not fail, if it continued, to become still more advantageous. In the course of a year, Law's notes rose to fifteen per cent premium, while the *billets d'état,* or notes issued by the government as security for the debts contracted by the extravagant Louis XIV., were at a discount of no less than seventy-eight and a half per cent. The comparison was too great in favour of Law not to attract the attention of the whole kingdom, and his credit extended itself day by day. Branches of his bank were almost simultaneously established at Lyons, Rochelle, Tours, Amiens, and Orleans.

The regent appears to have been utterly astonished at his success, and gradually to have conceived the idea that paper, which could so aid a metallic currency, could entirely supersede it. Upon this fundamental error he afterwards acted. In the mean time, Law commenced the famous project which has handed his name down to posterity. He proposed to the regent (who could refuse him nothing) to establish a company that should have the exclusive privilege of trading to the great river Mississippi and the province of Louisiana, on its western bank. The country was supposed to abound in the precious metals; and the company, supported by the profits of their exclusive commerce, were to be the sole farmers of the taxes and sole coiners of money. Letters patent were issued, incorporating the company, in August 1717. The capital was divided into two hundred thousand shares of five hundred livres each, the whole of which might be paid in *billets d'état,* at their nominal value, although worth no more than a hundred and sixty livres in the market.

It was now that the frenzy of speculating began to seize upon the nation. Law's bank had effected so much good, that any promises for the future which he thought proper to make were readily believed. The regent every day conferred new privileges upon the fortunate projector. The bank obtained the monopoly of the sale of tobacco, the sole right of refinage of gold and silver, and was finally erected into the Royal Bank of France. Amid the intoxication of success, both Law and the regent forgot the maxim so loudly proclaimed by the former, that a banker deserved death who made issues of paper without the necessary funds to provide for them. As soon as the bank, from a private, became a public institution, the regent caused a fabrication of notes to the amount of one thousand millions of livres. This was the first departure from sound principles, and one for which Law is not justly blameable. While the affairs of the bank were under his control, the issues had never exceeded sixty millions. Whether Law opposed the inordinate increase is not known; but as it took place as soon as the bank was made a royal establishment, it is but fair to lay the blame on the change of system upon the regent.

Law found that he lived under a despotic government; but he was not yet aware of the pernicious influence which such a government could exercise upon so delicate a framework as that of credit. He discovered it afterwards to his cost, but in the meantime suffered himself to be impelled by the regent into courses which his own reason must have disapproved. With a weakness most culpable, he lent his aid in inundating the country with paper money, which, based upon no solid foundation, was sure to fall, sooner or later. The extraordinary present fortune dazzled his eyes, and prevented him from seeing the evil day that would burst over his head, when once, from any cause or other, the alarm was sounded. The parliament were from the first jealous of his influence as a foreigner, and had, besides, their misgivings as to the safety of his projects. As his influence extended, their animosity increased. D'Aguesseau, the chancellor, was unceremoniously dismissed by the regent for his opposition to the vast increase of paper money, and the constant depreciation of the gold and silver coin of the realm. This only served to augment the enmity of the parliament, and when D'Argenson, a man devoted to the interests of the regent, was appointed to the vacant chancellorship, and made at the same time minister of finance, they became more violent than ever. The first measure of the new minister caused a further depreciation of the coin. In order to extinguish the *billets d'état,* it was ordered that persons bringing to the mint four thousand livres in specie and one thousand livres in *billets d'état,* should receive back coin to the amount of five thousand livres. D'Argenson plumed himself mightily upon thus creating five thousand new and smaller livres out of the four thousand old and larger ones, being too ignorant of the true principles of trade and credit to be aware of the immense injury he was inflicting upon both.

The parliament saw at once the impolicy and danger of such a system, and made repeated remonstrances to the regent. The latter refused to entertain their petitions, when the parliament, by a bold and very unusual stretch of authority, commanded that no money should be received in payment but that of the old standard. The regent summoned a *lit de justice,* and annulled the decree. The parliament resisted, and issued another. Again the regent exercised his privilege, and annulled it, till the parliament, stung to fiercer opposition, passed another decree, dated August 12th, 1718, by which they forbade the bank of Law to have any concern, either direct or indirect, in the administration of the revenue; and prohibited all foreigners, under heavy penalties, from interfering, either in their own names or in that of others, in the management of the finances of the state. The parliament considered Law to be the author of all the evil, and some of the councillors in the virulence of their enmity, proposed that he should be brought to trial, and, if found guilty, be hung at the gates of the Palais de Justice.

Law, in great alarm, fled to the Palais Royal, and threw himself on the protection of the regent, praying that measures might be taken to reduce the parliament to obedience. The regent had nothing so much at heart, both on that account and because of the disputes that had arisen relative to the legitimation of the Duke of Maine and the Count of Thoulouse, the sons of the late king. The parliament was ultimately overawed by the arrest of their president and two of the councillors, who were sent to distant prisons.

Thus the first cloud upon Law's prospects blew over: freed from apprehension of personal danger, he devoted his attention to his famous Mississippi project, the shares of which were rapidly rising, in spite of the parliament. At the commencement of the year 1719, an edict was published, granting to the Mississippi Company the exclusive privilege of trading to the East Indies, China, and the South Seas, and to all the possessions of the French East India Company, established by Colbert. The Company, in consequence of this great increase of their business, assumed, as more appropriate, the title of Company of the Indies, and created fifty thousand new shares. The prospects now held out by Law were most magnificent. He promised a yearly dividend of two hundred livres upon each share of five hundred, which, as the shares were paid for in *billets d'état*, at their nominal value, but worth only 100 livres, was at the rate of about 120 per cent profit.

The public enthusiasm, which had been so long rising, could not resist a vision so splendid. At least three hundred thousand applications were made for the fifty thousand new shares, and Law's house in the Rue de Quincampoix was beset from morning to night by the eager applicants. As it was impossible to satisfy them all, it was several weeks before a list of the fortunate new stockholders could be made out, during which time the public impatience rose to a pitch of frenzy. Dukes, marquises, counts, with their duchesses, marchionesses, and countesses, waited in the streets for hours every day before Mr. Law's door to know the result. At last, to avoid the jostling of the plebeian crowd, which, to the number of thousands, filled the whole thoroughfare, they took apartments in the adjoining houses, that they might be continually near the temple whence the new Plutus was diffusing wealth. Every day the value of the old shares increased, and the fresh applications, induced by the golden dreams of the whole nation, became so numerous that it was deemed advisable to create no less than three hundred thousand new shares, at five thousand livres each, in order that the regent might take advantage of the popular enthusiasm to pay off the national debt. For this purpose, the sum of fifteen hundred millions of livres was necessary. Such was the eagerness of the nation, that thrice the sum would have been subscribed if the government had authorised it.

Law was now at the zenith of his prosperity, and the people were rapidly approaching the zenith of their infatuation. The highest and the lowest classes were alike filled with a vision of boundless wealth. There was not a person of note among the aristocracy, with the exception of the Duke of St. Simon and Marshal Villars, who was not engaged in buying or selling stock. People of every age and sex and condition in life speculated in the rise and fall of the Mississippi bonds. The Rue de Quincampoix was the grand resort of the jobbers, and it being a narrow, inconvenient street, accidents continually occurred in it, from the tremendous pressure of the crowd. Houses in it, worth, in ordinary times, a thousand livres of yearly rent, yielded as much as twelve or sixteen thousand. A cobbler, who had a stall in it, gained about two hundred livres a day by letting it out, and furnishing writing materials to brokers and their clients. The story goes, that a hunchbacked man who stood in the street gained considerable sums by lending his hump as a writing-desk to the eager speculators! The great concourse of persons who assembled to do business brought a still greater concourse of spectators. These again drew all the thieves and immoral characters of Paris to the spot, and constant riots and disturbances took place. At nightfall, it was often found necessary to send a troop of soldiers to clear the street.

Law, finding the inconvenience of his residence, removed to the Place Vendôme, whither the crowd of *agioteurs* followed him. That spacious square soon became as thronged as the Rue de Quincampoix: from morning to night it presented the appearance of a fair. Booths and tents were erected for the transaction of business and the sale of refreshments, and gamblers with their roulette-tables stationed themselves in the very middle of the place, and reaped a golden, or rather a paper, harvest from the throng. The boulevards and public gardens were forsaken; parties of pleasure took their walks in preference in the Place Vendôme, which became the fashionable lounge of the idle as well as the general rendezvous of the busy. The noise was so great all day, that the chancellor, whose court was situated in the square, complained to the regent and the municipality that he could not hear the advocates. Law, when applied to, expressed his willingness to aid in the removal of the nuisance, and for this purpose entered into a treaty with the Prince de Carignan for the Hôtel de Soissons, which had a garden of several acres in the rear. A bargain was concluded, by which Law became the purchaser of the hotel at an enormous price, the prince reserving to himself the magnificent gardens as a new source of profit. They contained some fine statues and several fountains, and were altogether laid out with much taste. As soon as Law was installed in his new abode, an edict was published, forbidding all persons to buy or sell stock any where but in the gardens of the Hôtel de Soissons. In the midst, among the trees, about five hundred small tents and pavilions were erected, for the convenience of the stock-jobbers. Their various colours, the gay ribands and banners which floated from them, the busy crowds which passed continually in and out—the

37

incessant hum of voices, the noise, the music, and the strange mixture of business and pleasure on the countenances of the throng, all combined to give the place an air of enchantment that quite enraptured the Parisians. The Prince de Carignan made enormous profits while the delusion lasted. Each tent was let at the rate of five hundred livres a month; and, as there were at least five hundred of them, his monthly revenue from this source alone must have amounted to 250,000 livres, or upwards of 10,000*l.* sterling.

The honest old soldier, Marshal Villars, was so vexed to see the folly which had smitten his countrymen, that he never could speak with temper on the subject. Passing one day through the Place Vendôme in his carriage, the choleric gentleman was so annoyed at the infatuation of the people, that he abruptly ordered his coachman to stop, and, putting his head out of the carriage-window, harangued them for full half an hour on their "disgusting avarice." This was not a very wise proceeding on his part. Hisses and shouts of laughter resounded from every side, and jokes without number were aimed at him. There being at last strong symptoms that something more tangible was flying through the air in the direction of his head, the marshal was glad to drive on. He never again repeated the experiment.

Two sober, quiet, and philosophic men of letters, M. de la Motte and the Abbé Terrason, congratulated each other, that they, at least, were free from this strange infatuation. A few days afterward, as the worthy abbé was coming out of the Hôtel de Soissons, whither he had gone to buy shares in the Mississippi, whom should he see but his friend La Motte entering for the same purpose. "Ha!" said the abbé smiling, "is that *you?*" "Yes," said La Motte, pushing past him as fast as he was able; "and can that be *you?*" The next time the two scholars met, they talked of philosophy, of science, and of religion, but neither had courage for a long time to breathe one syllable about the Mississippi. At last, when it was mentioned, they agreed that a man ought never to swear against his doing any one thing, and that there was no sort of extravagance of which even a wise man was not capable.

During this time, Law, the new Plutus, had become all at once the most important personage of the state. The ante-chambers of the regent were forsaken by the courtiers. Peers, judges, and bishops thronged to the Hôtel de Soissons; officers of the army and navy, ladies of title and fashion, and every one to whom hereditary rank or public employ gave a claim to precedence, were to be found waiting in his ante-chambers to beg for a portion of his India stock. Law was so pestered that he was unable to see one-tenth part of the applicants, and every manœuvre that ingenuity could suggest was employed to gain access to him. Peers, whose dignity would have been outraged if the regent had made them wait half an hour for an interview, were content to wait six hours for the chance of seeing Monsieur Law. Enormous fees were paid to his servants, if they would merely announce their names. Ladies of rank employed the blandishments of their smiles for the same object; but many of them came day after day for a fortnight before they could obtain an audience. When Law accepted an invitation, he was sometimes so surrounded by ladies, all asking to have their names put down in his lists as shareholders in the new stock, that, in spite of his well-known and habitual gallantry, he was obliged to tear himself away *par force.* The most ludicrous stratagems were employed to have an opportunity of speaking to him. One lady, who had striven in vain during several days, gave up in despair all attempts to see him at his own house, but ordered her coachman to keep a strict watch whenever she was out in her carriage, and if he saw Mr. Law coming, to drive against a post and upset her. The coachman promised obedience, and for three days the lady was driven incessantly through the town, praying inwardly for the opportunity to be overturned. At last she espied Mr. Law, and, pulling the string, called out to the coachman, "Upset us now! for God's sake, upset us now!" The coachman drove against a post, the lady screamed, the coach was overturned, and Law, who had seen the *accident,* hastened to the spot to render assistance. The cunning dame was led into the Hôtel de Soissons, where she soon thought it advisable to recover from her fright, and, after apologizing to Mr. Law, confessed her stratagem. Law smiled, and entered the lady in his books as the purchaser of a quantity of India stock. Another story is told of a Madame de Boucha, who, knowing that Mr. Law was at dinner at a certain house, proceeded thither in her carriage, and gave the alarm of fire. The company started from table, and Law among the rest; but seeing one lady making all haste into the house towards him, while everybody else was scampering away, he suspected the trick, and ran off in another direction.

Many other anecdotes are related, which even though they may be a little exaggerated, are nevertheless worth preserving, as shewing the spirit of that singular period.* The regent was one day mentioning, in the presence of D'Argenson, the Abbé Dubois, and some other persons, that he was desirous of deputing some lady, of the rank at least of a duchess, to attend upon his daughter at Modena: "but," added he, "I do not exactly know where to find one." "No!" replied one, in affected surprise; "I can tell you where to find every duchess in France: you have only to go to Mr. Law's; you will see them every one in his ante-chamber."

M. de Chirac, a celebrated physician, had bought stock at an unlucky period, and was very anxious to sell out. Stock, however, continued to fall for two or three days, much to his alarm. His mind was filled with the subject, when he was suddenly called upon to attend a lady who imagined herself unwell. He arrived, was shewn up stairs, and felt the lady's pulse. "It falls! it falls! good God! it falls continually!" said he musingly, while the lady looked up in his face all anxiety for his opinion. "Oh, M. de Chirac," said she, starting to her feet and ringing the bell for assistance; "I am dying! I am dying! it falls! it falls! it falls!" "What falls?" inquired the doctor in amazement. "My pulse! my pulse!" said the lady; "I must be dying." "Calm your apprehensions, my dear madam," said M. de Chirac; "I was speaking of the stocks. The truth is, I have been a great loser, and my mind is so disturbed, I hardly know what I have been saying."

---

*The curious reader may find an anecdote of the eagerness of the French ladies to retain Law in their company, which will make him blush or smile according as he happens to be very modest or the reverse. It is related in the *Letters of Madame Charlotte Elizabeth de Bavière, Duchess of Orleans*, vol. ii, p. 274.

The price of shares sometimes rose ten or twenty per cent in the course of a few hours, and many persons in the humbler walks of life, who had risen poor in the morning, went to bed in affluence. An extensive holder of stock, being taken ill, sent his servant to sell two hundred and fifty shares, at eight thousand livres each, the price at which they were then quoted. The servant went, and, on his arrival in the Jardin de Soissons, found that in the interval the price had risen to ten thousand livres. The difference of two thousand livres on the two hundred and fifty shares, amounting to 500,000 livres, or 20,000*l.* sterling, he very coolly transferred to his own use, and giving the remainder to his master, set out the same evening for another country. Law's coachman in a very short time made money enough to set up a carriage of his own, and requested permission to leave his service. Law, who esteemed the man, begged of him as a favour that he would endeavour, before he went, to find a substitute as good as himself. The coachman consented, and in the evening brought two of his former comrades, telling Mr. Law to choose between them, and he would take the other. Cookmaids and footmen were now and then as lucky, and, in the full-blown pride of their easily-acquired wealth, made the most ridiculous mistakes. Preserving the language and manners of their old with the finery of their new station, they afforded continual subjects for the pity of the sensible, the contempt of the sober, and the laughter of everybody. But the folly and meanness of the higher ranks of society were still more disgusting. One instance alone, related by the Duke de St. Simon, will shew the unworthy avarice which infected the whole of society. A man of the name of André, without character or education, had, by a series of well-timed speculations in Mississippi bonds, gained enormous wealth in an incredibly short space of time. As St. Simon expresses it, "he had amassed mountains of gold." As he became rich, he grew ashamed of the lowness of his birth, and anxious above all things to be allied to nobility. He had a daughter, an infant only three years of age, and he opened a negotiation with the aristocratic and needy family of D'Oyse, that this child should, upon certain conditions, marry a member of that house. The Marquis D'Oyse, to his shame, consented, and promised to marry her himself on her attaining the age of twelve, if the father would pay him down the sum of a hundred thousand crowns, and twenty thousand livres every year until the celebration of the marriage. The Marquis was himself in his thirty-third year. This scandalous bargain was duly signed and sealed, the stockjobber furthermore agreeing to settle upon his daughter, on the marriage-day, a fortune of several millions. The Duke of Brancas, the head of the family, was present throughout the negotiation, and shared in all the profits. St. Simon, who treats the matter with the levity becoming what he thought so good a joke, adds, "that people did not spare their animadversions of this beautiful marriage," and further informs us "that the project fell to the ground some months afterwards by the overthrow of Law, and the ruin of the ambitious Monsieur André." It would appear, however, that the noble family never had the honesty to return the hundred thousand crowns.

Amid events like these, which, humiliating though they be, partake largely of the ludicrous, others occurred of a more serious nature. Robberies in the streets were of daily occurrence, in consequence of the immense sums, in paper, which people carried about with them. Assassinations were also frequent. One case in particular fixed the attention of the whole of France, not only on account of the enormity of the offence, but of the rank and high connexions of the criminal.

The Count d'Horn, a younger brother of the Prince d'Horn, and related to the noble families of D'Aremberg, DeLigne, and DeMontmorency, was a young man of dissipated character, extravagant to a degree, and unprincipled as he was extravagant. In connexion with two other young men as reckless as himself, named Mille, a Piedmontese captain, and one Destampes, or Lestang, a Fleming, he formed a design to rob a very rich broker, who was known, unfortunately for himself, to carry great sums about his person. The count pretended a desire to purchase of him a number of shares in the Company of the Indies, and for that purpose appointed to meet him in a *cabaret*, or low public-house, in the neighbourhood of the Place Vendôme. The unsuspecting broker was punctual to his appointment; so were the Count d'Horn and his two associates, whom he introduced as his particular friends. After a few moments' conversation, the Count d'Horn suddenly sprang upon his victim, and stabbed him three times in the breast with a poniard. The man fell heavily to the ground, and, while the count was employed in rifling his portfolio of bonds in the Mississippi and Indian schemes to the amount of one hundred thousand crowns, Mille, the Piedmontese, stabbed the unfortunate broker again and again, to make sure of his death. But the broker did not fall without a struggle, and his cries brought the people of the *cabaret* to his assistance. Lestang, the other assassin, who had been set to keep watch at a staircase, sprang from a window and escaped; but Mille and the Count d'Horn were seized in the very act.

This crime, committed in open day, and in so public a place as a *cabaret*, filled Paris with consternation. The trial of the assassins commenced on the following day; and the evidence being so clear, they were both found guilty, and condemned to be broken alive on the wheel. The noble relatives of the Count d'Horn absolutely blocked up the ante-chambers of the regent, praying for mercy on the misguided youth, and alleging that he was insane. The regent avoided them as long as possible, being determined that, in a case so atrocious, justice should take its course. But the importunity of these influential suitors was not to be overcome so silently; and they at last forced themselves into the presence of the regent, and prayed him to save their house the shame of a public execution. They hinted that the Princes d'Horn were allied to the illustrious family of Orleans; and added, that the regent himself would be disgraced if a kinsman of his should die by the hands of a common executioner. The regent, to his credit, was proof against all their solicitations, and replied to their last argument in the words of Corneille:

"Le crime fait la honte, et non pas l'échafaud:"

adding, that whatever shame there might be in the punishment he would very willingly share with the other relatives. Day after day they renewed their entreaties, but always with the same result. At last they thought, that if they could interest the Duke de St. Simon in their favour—a man for whom the regent felt sincere esteem—they might succeed in their object. The duke, a thorough aristocrat, was as shocked as they were that a noble assassin should die by the same death as a plebeian felon, and represented to the regent the impolicy of making enemies of so numerous, wealthy, and powerful a family. He urged, too, that in Germany, where the family of D'Aremberg had large possessions, it was the law, that no relative of a person broken on the wheel could succeed to any public office or employ until a whole generation had passed away. For this reason, he thought the punishment of the guilty might be transmuted into beheading, which was considered all over Europe as much less infamous. The regent was moved by this argument, and was about to consent, when Law, who felt peculiarly interested in the fate of the murdered man, confirmed him in his former resolution to let the law take its course.

The relatives of D'Horn were now reduced to the last extremity. The Prince de Robec Montmorency, despairing of other methods, found means to penetrate into the dungeon of the criminal, and offering him a cup of poison, implored him to save them from disgrace. The Count d'Horn turned away his head, and refused to take it. Montmorency pressed him once more; and losing all patience at his continued refusal, turned on his heel, and exclaiming, "Die, then, as thou wilt, mean-spirited wretch! thou art fit only to perish by the hands of the hangman!" left him to his fate.

D'Horn himself petitioned the regent that he might be beheaded; but Law, who exercised more influence over his mind than any other person, with the exception of the notorious Abbé Dubois, his tutor, insisted that he could not in justice succumb to the self-interested views of the D'Horns. The regent had from the first been of the same opinion: and within six days after the commission of their crime, D'Horn and Mille were broken on the wheel in the Place de Grève. The other assassin, Lestang, was never apprehended.

This prompt and severe justice was highly pleasing to the populace of Paris. Even M. de Quincampoix, as they called Law, came in for a share of their approbation for having induced the regent to show no favour to a patrician. But the number of robberies and assassinations did not diminish; no sympathy was shewn for rich jobbers when they were plundered. The general laxity of public morals, conspicuous enough before, was rendered still more so by its rapid pervasion of the middle classes, who had hitherto remained comparatively pure between the open vices of the class above and the hidden crimes of the class below them. The pernicious love of gambling diffused itself through society, and bore all public and nearly all private virtue before it.

For a time, while confidence lasted, an impetus was given to trade which could not fail to be beneficial. In Paris especially the good results were felt. Strangers flocked into the capital from every part, bent not only upon making money, but on spending it. The Duchess of Orleans, mother of the regent, computes the increase of the population during this time, from the great influx of strangers from all parts of the world, at 305,000 souls. The housekeepers were obliged to make up beds in garrets, kitchens, and even stables, for the accommodation of lodgers; and the town was so full of carriages and vehicles of every description, that they were obliged, in the principal streets, to drive at a foot-pace for fear of accidents. The looms of the country worked with unusual activity to supply rich laces, silks, broad-cloth, and velvets, which being paid for in abundant paper, increased in price fourfold. Provisions shared the general advance. Bread, meat, and vegetables were sold at prices greater than had ever before been known; while the wages of labour rose in exactly the same proportion. The artisan who formerly gained fifteen sous per diem now gained sixty. New houses were built in every direction; an illusory prosperity shone over the land, and so dazzled the eyes of the whole nation, that none could see the dark cloud on the horizon announcing the storm that was too rapidly approaching.

Law himself, the magician whose wand had wrought so surprising a change, shared, of course, in the general prosperity. His wife and daughter were courted by the highest nobility, and their alliance sought by the heirs of ducal and princely houses. He bought two splendid estates in different parts of France, and entered into a negotiation with the family of the Duke de Sully for the purchase of the marquisate of Rosny. His religion being an obstacle to his advancement, the regent promised, if he would publicly conform to the Catholic faith, to make him comptroller-general of the finances. Law, who had no more real religion than any other professed gambler, readily agreed, and was confirmed by the Abbé de Tencin in the cathedral of Melun, in presence of a great crowd of spectators.* On the following day he was elected honorary church-warden of the parish of St. Roch, upon which occasion he made it a present of the sum of five hundred thousand livres. His charities, always magnificent, were not always so ostentatious. He gave away great sums privately, and no tale of real distress ever reached his ears in vain.

At this time he was by far the most influential person of the state. The Duke of Orleans had so much confidence in his sagacity and the success of his plans, that he always consulted him upon every matter of moment. He was by no means unduly elevated by his prosperity, but remained the same simple,

---

* The following squib was circulated on the occasion:

> "Foin de ton zèle séraphique,
>   Malheureux Abbé de Tencin,
> Depuis que Law est Catholique,
>   Tout le royaume est Capucin!"

Thus somewhat weakly and paraphrastically rendered by Justandsond, in his translation of the *Memoirs of Louis XV.:*

> "Tencin, a curse on thy seraphic zeal,
>   Which by persuasion hath contrived the means
> To make the Scotchman at our altars kneel,
>   Since which we all are poor as Capucines!"

affable, sensible man that he had shewn himself in adversity. His gallantry, which was always delightful to the fair objects of it, was of a nature so kind, so gentlemanly, and so respectful, that not even a lover could have taken offence at it. If upon any occasion he showed any symptoms of haughtiness, it was to the cringing nobles who lavished their adulation upon him till it became fulsome. He often took pleasure in seeing how long he could make them dance attendance upon him for a single favour. To such of his own countrymen as by chance visited Paris, and sought an interview with him, he was, on the contrary, all politeness and attention. When Archibald Campbell, Earl of Islay, and afterwards Duke of Argyle, called upon him in the Place Vendôme, he had to pass through an ante-chamber crowded with persons of the first distinction, all anxious to see the great financier, and have their names put down as first on the list of some new subscription. Law himself was quietly sitting in his library, writing a letter to the gardener at his paternal estate of Lauriston, about the planting of some cabbages! The earl stayed a considerable time, played a game of piquet with his countryman, and left him charmed with his ease, good sense, and good breeding.

Among the nobles who, by means of the public credulity at this time, gained sums sufficient to repair their ruined fortunes, may be mentioned the names of the Dukes de Bourbon, de Guiche, de la Force,* de Chaulnes, and d'Antin; the Maréchal d'Estrées; the Princes de Rohan, de Poix, and de Léon. The Duke de Bourbon, son of Louis XIV. by Madame de Montespan, was peculiarly fortunate in his speculations in Mississippi paper. He rebuilt the royal residence of Chantilly in a style of unwonted magnificence; and being passionately fond of horses, he erected a range of stables, which were long renowned

---

* The Duke de la Force gained considerable sums, not only by jobbing in the stocks but in dealing in porcelain, spices, &c. It was debated for a length of time in the parliament of Paris whether he had not, in his quality of spice-merchant, forfeited his rank in the peerage. It was decided in the negative. A caricature of him was made, dressed as a street-porter, carrying a large bale of spices on his back, with the inscription, "Admirez LA FORCE."

throughout Europe, and imported a hundred and fifty of the finest racers from England to improve the breed in France. He bought a large extent of country in Picardy, and became possessed of nearly all the valuable lands lying between the Oise and the Somme.

When fortunes such as these were gained, it is no wonder that Law should have been almost worshipped by the mercurial population. Never was monarch more flattered than he was. All the small poets and *littérateurs* of the day poured floods of adulation upon him. According to them, he was the saviour of the country, the tutelary divinity of France; wit was in all his words, goodness in all his looks, and wisdom in all his actions. So great a crowd followed his carriage whenever he went abroad, that the regent sent him a troop of horse as his permanent escort to clear the streets before him.

It was remarked at this time that Paris had never before been so full of objects of elegance and luxury. Statues, pictures, and tapestries were imported in great quantities from foreign countries, and found a ready market. All those pretty trifles in the way of furniture and ornament which the French excel in manufacturing were no longer the exclusive playthings of the aristocracy, but were to be found in abundance in the houses of traders and the middle classes in general. Jewellery of the most costly description was brought to Paris as the most favourable mart; among the rest, the famous diamond bought by the regent, and called by his name, and which long adorned the crown of France. It was purchased for the sum of two millions of livres, under circumstances which shew that the regent was not so great a gainer as some of his subjects by the impetus which trade had received. When the diamond was first offered to him, he refused to buy it, although he desired above all things to possess it, alleging as his reason, that his duty to the country he governed would not allow him to spend so large a sum of the public money for a mere jewel. This valid and honourable excuse threw all the ladies of the court into alarm, and nothing was heard for some days but expressions of regret that so rare a gem should be allowed to go out of France, no private individual being rich enough to buy it. The regent was continually importuned about it, but all in vain, until the Duke de St. Simon, who with all his ability, was something of a twaddler, undertook the weighty business. His entreaties being seconded by Law, the good-natured regent gave his consent, leaving to Law's ingenuity to find the means to pay for it. The owner took security for the payment of the sum of two millions of livres within a stated period, receiving in the mean time the interest of five per cent upon that amount, and being allowed, besides, all the valuable clippings of the gem. St. Simon, in his *Memoirs,* relates with no little complacency his share in this transaction. After describing the diamond to be as large as a greengage, of a form nearly round, perfectly white, and without flaw, and weighing more than five hundred grains, he concludes with a chuckle, by telling the world "that he takes great credit to himself for having induced the regent to make so illustrious a purchase." In other words, he was proud that he had induced him to sacrifice his duty, and buy a bauble for himself at an extravagant price out of the public money.

Thus the system continued to flourish till the commencement of the year 1720. The warnings of the Parliament, that too great a creation of paper money would, sooner or later, bring the country to bankruptcy, were disregarded. The regent, who knew nothing whatever of the philosophy of finance, thought that a system which had produced such good effects could never be carried to excess. If five hundred millions of paper had been of such advantage, five hundred millions additional would be of still greater advantage. This was the grand error of the regent, and which Law did not attempt to dispel. The extraordinary avidity of the people kept up the delusion; and the higher the price of Indian and Mississippi stock, the more *billets de banque* were issued to keep pace with it. The edifice thus reared might not unaptly be compared to the gorgeous palace erected by Potemkin, that princely barbarian of Russia, to surprise and please his imperial mistress: huge blocks of ice were piled one upon another; Ionic pillars of chastest workmanship, in ice, formed a noble portico; and a dome of the same material, shone in the sun, which had just strength enough to gild, but not to melt it. It glittered afar, like a palace of crystals and diamonds; but there came one warm breeze from the south, and the stately building dissolved away, till none were able even to gather up the fragments. So with Law and his paper system. No sooner did the breath of popular mistrust blow steadily upon it, than it fell to ruins, and none could raise it up again.

The first slight alarm that was occasioned was early in 1720. The Prince de Conti, offended that Law should have denied him fresh shares in India stock, at his own price, sent to his bank to demand payment in specie of so enormous a quantity of notes, that three waggons were required for its transport. Law complained to the regent, and urged on his attention the mischief that would be done, if such an example found many imitators. The regent was but too well aware of it, and, sending for the Prince de Conti, ordered him, under penalty of his high displeasure, to refund to the bank two-thirds of the specie which he had withdrawn from it. The prince was forced to obey the despotic mandate. Happily for Law's credit, De Conti was an unpopular man: everybody condemned his meanness and cupidity, and agreed that Law had been hardly treated. It is strange, however, that so narrow an escape should not have made both Law and the regent more anxious to restrict their issues. Others were soon found who imitated from motives of distrust, the example which had been set by De Conti in revenge. The more acute stockjobbers imagined justly that prices could not continue to rise for ever. Bourdon and La Richardière, renowned for their extensive operations in the funds, quietly and in small quantities at a time, converted their notes into specie, and sent it away to foreign countries. They also bought as much as they could conveniently carry of plate and expensive jewellery, and sent it secretly away to England or to Holland. Vermalet, a jobber, who sniffed the coming storm, procured gold and silver coin to the amount of nearly a million of livres, which he packed in a farmer's cart, and covered over with hay and cow-dung. He then disguised himself in the dirty smock-frock, or *blouse,* of a peasant, and drove his precious load in safety into Belgium. From thence he soon found means to transport it to Amsterdam.

Hitherto no difficulty had been experienced by any class in procuring specie for their wants. But this system could not long be carried on without causing a scarcity. The voice of complaint was heard on every side, and inquiries being instituted, the cause was soon discovered. The council debated long on the remedies to be taken, and Law, being called on for his advice, was of opinion, that an edict should be published, depreciating the value of coin five per cent below that of paper. The edict was published accordingly; but failing of its intended effect, was followed by another, in which the depreciation was increased to ten per cent. The payments of the bank were at the same time restricted to one hundred livres in gold, and ten in silver. All these measures were nugatory to restore confidence in the paper, though the restriction of cash payments within limits so extremely narrow kept up the credit of the bank.

Notwithstanding every effort to the contrary, the precious metals continued to be conveyed to England and Holland. The little coin that was left in the country was carefully treasured, or hidden until the scarcity became so great, that the operations of trade could no longer be carried on. In this emergency, Law hazarded the bold experiment of forbidding the use of specie altogether. In February 1720 an edict was published, which, instead of restoring the credit of the paper, as was intended, destroyed it irrecoverably, and drove the country to the very brink of revolution. By this famous edict it was forbidden to any person whatever to have more than five hundred livres (20*l.*) of coin in his possession, under pain of a heavy fine, and confiscation of the sums found. It was also forbidden to buy up jewellery, plate, and precious stones, and informers were encouraged to make search for offenders, by the promise of one-half the amount they might discover. The whole country sent up a cry of distress at this unheard-of tyranny. The most odious persecution daily took place. The privacy of families was

51

violated by the intrusion of informers and their agents. The most virtuous and honest were denounced for the crime of having been seen with a *louis d'or* in their possession. Servants betrayed their masters, one citizen became a spy upon his neighbour, and arrests and confiscations so multiplied, that the courts found a difficulty in getting through the immense increase of business thus occasioned. It was sufficient for an informer to say that he suspected any person of concealing money in his house, and immediately a search-warrant was granted. Lord Stair, the English ambassador, said, that it was now impossible to doubt of the sincerity of Law's conversion to the Catholic religion; he had established the *inquisition,* after having given abundant evidence of his faith in *transubstantiation,* by turning so much gold into paper.

Every epithet that popular hatred could suggest was showered upon the regent and the unhappy Law. Coin, to any amount above five hundred livres, was an illegal tender, and nobody would take paper if he could help it. No one knew to-day what his notes would be worth to-morrow. "Never," says Duclos, in his *Secret Memoirs of the Regency,* "was seen a more capricious government—never was a more frantic tyranny exercised by hands less firm. It is inconceivable to those who were witnesses of the horrors of those times, and who look back upon them now as on a dream, that a sudden revolution did not break out—that Law and the regent did not perish by a tragical death. They were both held in horror, but the people confined themselves to complaints; a sombre and timid despair, a stupid consternation, had seized upon all, and men's minds were too vile even to be capable of a courageous crime." It would appear that, at one time, a movement of the people was organised. Seditious writings were posted up against the walls, and were sent, in hand-bills, to the houses of the most conspicuous people. One of them, given in the *Mémoires de la Régence,* was to the following effect:—"Sir and madam,—This is to give you notice that a St. Bartholomew's Day will be enacted again on Saturday and Sunday, if affairs do not alter. You are desired not to stir out, nor you, nor your servants. God preserve you from the flames! Give notice to your neighbours. Dated, Saturday, May 25th, 1720." The immense number of spies with which the city was infested rendered the people mistrustful of one another, and beyond some trifling disturbances made in the evening by an insignificant group, which was soon dispersed, the peace of the capital was not compromised.

The value of shares in the Louisiana, or Mississippi stock, had fallen very rapidly, and few indeed were found to believe the tales that had once been told of the immense wealth of that region. A last effort was therefore tried to restore the public confidence in the Mississippi project. For this purpose, a general conscription of all the poor wretches in Paris was made by order of government. Upwards of six thousand of the very refuse of the population were impressed, as if in time of war, and were provided with clothes and tools to be embarked for New Orleans, to work in the gold mines alleged to abound there. They were paraded day after day through the streets with their pikes and shovels, and then sent off in small detachments to the out-ports to be shipped for America. Two-thirds of them never reached their destination, but dispersed themselves over the country, sold their tools for what they could get, and returned to their old course of life. In less than three weeks afterwards, one-half of them were to be found again in Paris. The manœuvre, however, caused a trifling advance in Mississippi stock. Many persons of superabundant gullibility believed that operations had begun in earnest in the new Golconda, and that gold and silver ingots would again be found in France.

In a constitutional monarchy some surer means would have been found for the restoration of public credit. In England, at a subsequent period, when a similar delusion had brought on similar distress, how different were the measures taken to repair the evil! but in France, unfortunately, the remedy was left to the authors of the mischief. The arbitrary will of the regent, which endeavoured to extricate the country, only plunged it deeper into the mire. All payments were ordered to be made in paper, and between the 1st of February and the end of May, notes were fabricated to the amount of upwards of 1500 millions of livres, or 60,000,000*l.* sterling. But the alarm once sounded, no art could make the people feel the slightest confidence in paper which was not exchangeable into metal. M. Lambert, the president of the parliament of Paris, told the regent to his face that he would rather have a hundred thousand livres in gold or silver than five millions in the notes of his bank. When such was the general feeling, the superabundant issues of paper but increased the evil, by rendering still more enormous the disparity between the amount of specie and notes in circulation. Coin, which it was the object of the regent to depreciate, rose in value on every fresh attempt to diminish it. In February, it was judged advisable that the Royal Bank should be incorporated with the Company of the Indies. An edict to that effect was published and registered by the parliament. The state remained the guarantee for the notes of the bank, and no more were to be issued without an order in council. All the profits of the bank, since the time it had been taken out of Law's hands and made a national institution, were given over by the regent to the Company of the Indies. This measure had the effect of raising for a short time the value of the Louisiana and other shares of the company, but it failed in placing public credit on any permanent basis.

A council of state was held in the beginning of May, at which Law, D'Argenson (his colleague in the administration of the finances), and all the ministers were present. It was then computed that the total amount of notes in circulation was 2600 millions of livres, while the coin in the country was not quite equal to half that amount. It was evident to the majority of the council that some plan must be adopted to equalize the currency. Some proposed that the notes should be reduced to the value of the specie, while others proposed that the nominal value of the specie should be raised till it was on an equality with the paper. Law is said to have opposed both these projects, but failing in suggesting any other, it was agreed that the notes should be depreciated one half. On the 21st of May, an edict was accordingly issued, by which it was decreed that the shares of the Company of the Indies, and the notes of the bank, should gradually diminish in value, till at the end of a year they should only pass current for one-half of their nominal worth. The parliament refused to register the edict—the greatest outcry was excited, and the state of the country became so alarming, that, as the only means of preserving tranquillity, the council of the regency was obliged to stultify its own proceedings, by publishing within seven days another edict, restoring the notes to their original value.

On the same day (the 27th of May) the bank stopped payment in specie. Law and D'Argenson were both dismissed from the ministry. The weak, vacillating, and cowardly regent threw the blame of all the mischief upon Law, who, upon presenting himself at the Palais Royal, was refused admittance. At nightfall, however, he was sent for, and admitted into the palace by a secret door,* when the regent endeavoured to console him, and made all manner of excuses for the severity with which in public he had been compelled to treat him. So capricious was his conduct, that, two days afterwards, he took him publicly to the opera, where he sat in the royal box alongside of the regent, who treated him with marked consideration in face of all the people. But such was the hatred against Law that the experiment had well nigh proved fatal to him. The mob assailed his carriage with stones just as he was entering his own door; and if the coachman had not made a sudden jerk into the courtyard, and the domestics closed the gate immediately, he would, in all probability, have been dragged out and torn to pieces. On the following day, his wife and daughter were also assailed by the mob as they were returning in their carriage from the races. When the regent was informed of these occurrences he sent Law a strong detachment of Swiss guards, who were stationed night and day in the court of his residence. The public indignation at last increased so much, that Law, finding his own house, even with this guard, insecure, took refuge in the Palais Royal, in the apartments of the regent.

---

* Duclos, *Mémoires Secrets de la Régence.*

The Chancellor, D'Aguesseau, who had been dismissed in 1718 for his opposition to the projects of Law, was now recalled to aid in the restoration of credit. The regent acknowledged too late, that he had treated with unjustifiable harshness and mistrust one of the ablest, and perhaps the sole honest public man of that corrupt period. He had retired ever since his disgrace to his country house at Fresnes, where, in the midst of severe but delightful philosophic studies, he had forgotten the intrigues of an unworthy court. Law himself, and the Chevalier de Conflans, a gentleman of the regent's household, were despatched in a post-chaise with orders to bring the ex-chancellor to Paris along with them. D'Aguesseau consented to render what assistance he could, contrary to the advice of his friends, who did not approve that he should accept any recall to office of which Law was the bearer. On his arrival in Paris, five councillors of the parliament were admitted to confer with the Commissary of Finance; and on the 1st of June an order was published abolishing the law which made it criminal to amass coin to the amount of more than five hundred livres. Every one was permitted to have as much specie as he pleased. In order that the bank-notes might be withdrawn, twenty-five millions of new notes were created, on the security of the revenues of the city of Paris, at two and a half per cent. The bank-notes withdrawn were publicly burned in front of the Hôtel de Ville. The new notes were principally of the value of ten livres each; and on the 10th of June the bank was re-opened, with a sufficiency of silver coin to give in change for them.

These measures were productive of considerable advantage. All the population of Paris hastened to the bank to get coin for their small notes; and silver becoming scarce, they were paid in copper. Very few complained that this was too heavy, although poor fellows might be continually seen toiling and sweating along the streets, laden with more than they could comfortably carry, in the shape of change for fifty livres. The crowds around the bank were so great that hardly a day passed that some one was not pressed to death. On the 9th of

July, the multitude was so dense and clamorous that the guards stationed at the entrance of the Mazarin Gardens closed the gate and refused to admit any more. The crowd became incensed, and flung stones through the railings upon the soldiers. The latter, incensed in their turn, threatened to fire upon the people. At that instant one of them was hit by a stone, and, taking up his piece, he fired into the crowd. One man fell dead immediately, and another was severely wounded. It was every instant expected that a general attack would have been commenced upon the bank; but the gates of the Mazarin Gardens being opened to the crowd, who saw a whole troop of soldiers, with their bayonets fixed ready to receive them, they contented themselves by giving vent to their indignation in groans and hisses.

Eight days afterwards the concourse of people was so tremendous that fifteen persons were squeezed to death at the doors of the bank. The people were so indignant that they took three of the bodies on stretchers before them, and proceeded, to the number of seven or eight thousand, to the gardens of the Palais Royal, that they might show the regent the misfortunes that he and Law had brought upon the country. Law's coachman, who was sitting on the box of his master's carriage, in the court-yard of the palace, happened to have more zeal than discretion, and, not liking that the mob should abuse his master, he said, loud enough to be overheard by several persons, that they were all blackguards, and deserved to be hanged. The mob immediately set upon him, and thinking that Law was in the carriage, broke it to pieces. The imprudent coachman narrowly escaped with his life. No further mischief was done; a body of troops making their appearance, the crowd quietly dispersed, after an assurance had been given by the regent that the three bodies they had brought to shew him should be decently buried at his own expense. The parliament was sitting at the time of this uproar, and the president took upon himself to go out and see what was the matter. On his return he informed the councillors that Law's carriage had been broken by the mob. All the members rose simultaneously, and expressed their joy by a loud shout, while one man, more zealous in his hatred than the rest, exclaimed, *"And Law himself, is he torn to pieces?"**

Much, undoubtedly, depended on the credit of the Company of the Indies, which was answerable for so great a sum to the nation. It was therefore suggested in the council of the ministry, that any privileges which could be granted to enable it to fulfil its engagements, would be productive of the best results. With this end in view, it was proposed that the exclusive privilege of all maritime commerce should be secured to it, and an edict to that effect was published. But it was unfortunately forgotten that by such a measure all the merchants of the country would be ruined. The idea of such an immense privilege was generally scouted by the nation, and petition on petition was presented to the parliament that they would refuse to register the decree. They refused accordingly, and the regent, remarking that they did nothing but fan the flame of sedition, exiled them to Blois. At the intercession of D'Aguesseau, the place of banishment was changed to Pontoise, and thither accordingly the councillors repaired, determined to set the regent at defiance. They made every arrangement for rendering their temporary exile as agreeable as possible. The president gave the most elegant suppers, to which he invited all the gayest and wittiest company of Paris. Every night there was a concert and ball for the ladies. The usually grave and solemn judges and councillors joined in cards and other diversions, leading for several weeks a life of the most extravagant pleasure, for no other purpose than to show the regent of how little consequence they deemed their

---

* The Duchess of Orleans gives a different version of this story; but whichever be the true one, the manifestation of such feeling in a legislative assembly was not very creditable. She says that the president was so transported with joy, that he was seized with a rhyming fit, and returning into the hall, exclaimed to the members:

"Messieurs! Messieurs! bonne nouvelle!
Le carrosse de Lass est reduit en cannelle!"

banishment, and that, when they willed it, they could make Pontoise a pleasanter residence than Paris.

Of all the nations in the world the French are the most renowned for singing over their grievances. Of that country it has been remarked with some truth, that its whole history may be traced in its songs. When Law, by the utter failure of his best-laid plans, rendered himself obnoxious, satire of course seized hold upon him; and while caricatures of his person appeared in all the shops, the streets resounded with songs, in which neither he nor the regent was spared. Many of these songs were far from decent; and one of them in particular counselled the application of all his notes to the most ignoble use to which paper can be applied. But the following, preserved in the letters of the Duchess of Orleans, was the best and the most popular, and was to be heard for months in all the *carrefours* in Paris. The application of the chorus is happy enough:

> Aussitôt que Lass arriva
> Dans notre bonne ville,
> Monsieur le Régent publia
> Que Lass serait utile
> Pour rétablir la nation.
> *La faridondaine! la faridondon!*
> Mais il nous a tous enrichi,
>   *Biribi!*
> *A la façon de Barbari,*
>   *Mon ami*

> Ce parpaillot, pour attirer
> Tout l'argent de la France,
> Songea d'abord à s'assurer
> De notre confiance.
> Il fit son abjuration,
> *La faridondaine! la faridondon!*
> Mais le fourbe s'est converti,
>   *Biribi!*
> *A la façon de Barbari,*
>   *Mon ami!*

Lass, le fils aîné de Satan
  Nous met tous à l'aumône,
Il nous a pris tout notre argent
  Et n'en rend à personne.
Mais le Régent, humain et bon,
  La faridondaine! la faridondon!
    Nous rendra ce qu'on nous a pris,
      Biribi!
A la façon de Barbari,
      Mon ami!

The following epigram is of the same date:

Lundi, j'achetai des actions;
Mardi, je gagnai des millions;
Mercredi, j'arrangeai mon ménage,
Jeudi, je pris un équipage,
Vendredi, je m'en fus au bal,
Et Samedi, à l'hôpital.

Among the caricatures that were abundantly published, and that shewed as plainly as graver matters that the nation had awakened to a sense of its folly, was one, a fac-simile of which is preserved in the *Mémoires de la Régence*. It was thus described by its author: "The 'Goddess of Shares,' in her triumphal car, driven by the Goddess of Folly. Those who are drawing the car are impersonations of the Mississippi, with his wooden leg, the South Sea, the Bank of England, the Company of the West of Senegal, and of various assurances. Lest the car should not roll fast enough, the agents of these companies, known by their long fox-tails and their cunning looks, turn round the spokes of the wheels, upon which are marked the names of the several stocks and their value, sometimes high and sometimes low, according to the turns of the wheel. Upon the ground are the merchandise, day-books and ledgers of legitimate commerce, crushed under the chariot of Folly. Behind is an immense crowd of persons, of all ages, sexes, and conditions, clamouring after Fortune, and fighting with each other to get a portion of the shares which she distributes so bountifully among them. In the clouds sits a demon, blowing bubbles of soap, which are also the objects of the admiration and cupidity of the crowd, who jump upon one another's backs to reach them ere they burst. Right in the pathway of the car, and blocking up the passage, stands a large building, with three doors, through one of which it must pass, if it proceeds farther, and all the crowd along with it. Over the first door are the words, '*Hôpital des Foux,*' over the second, '*Hôpital des Malades,*' and over the third, '*Hôpital des Gueux.*'" Another caricature represented Law sitting in a large cauldron, boiling over the flames of popular madness, surrounded by an impetuous multitude, who were pouring all their gold and silver into it, and receiving gladly in exchange the bits of paper which he distributed among them by handfuls.

While this excitement lasted, Law took good care not to expose himself unguarded in the streets. Shut up in the apartments of the regent, he was secure from all attack; and whenever he ventured abroad, it was either *incognito,* or in one of the royal carriages, with a powerful escort. An amusing anecdote is recorded of the detestation in which he was held by the people, and the ill-treatment he would have met had he fallen into their hands. A gentleman of the name of Boursel was passing in his carriage down the Rue St. Antoine, when his farther progress was stayed by a hackney-coach that had blocked up the road. M. Boursel's servant called impatiently to the hackney-coachman to get out of the way, and, on his refusal, struck him a blow on the face. A crowd was soon drawn together by the disturbance, and M. Boursel got out of the carriage to restore order. The hackney-coachman, imagining that he had now another assailant, bethought him of an expedient to rid himself of both, and called out as loudly as he was able, "Help! help! murder! murder! Here are Law and his servant going to kill me! Help! help!" At this cry the people came out of their shops, armed with sticks and other weapons, while the mob gathered stones to inflict summary vengeance upon the supposed financier. Happily for M. Boursel and his servant, the door of the church of the Jesuits stood wide open, and, seeing the fearful odds against them, they rushed towards it with all speed. They reached the altar, pursued by the people, and would have been ill-treated even there if, finding the door open leading to the sacristy, they had not sprang through, and closed it after them. The mob were then persuaded to leave the church by the alarmed and indignant priests, and finding M. Boursel's carriage still in the streets, they vented their ill-will against it, and did it considerable damage.

The twenty-five millions secured on the municipal revenues of the city of Paris, bearing so low an interest as two and a half per cent, were not very popular among the large holders of Mississippi stock. The conversion of the securities was, therefore, a work of considerable difficulty; for many preferred to retain the falling paper of Law's company, in the hope that a favourable turn might take place. On the 15th of August, with a view to hasten the conversion, an edict was passed, declaring that all notes for sums between one thousand and ten thousand livres should not pass current, except for the purchase of annuities and bank accounts, or for the payment of instalments still due on the shares of the company.

In October following another edict was passed, depriving these notes of all value whatever after the month of November next ensuing. The management of the mint, the farming of the revenue, and all the other advantages and privileges of the India, or Mississippi Company, were taken from them, and they were reduced to a mere private company. This was the death-blow to the whole system, which had now got into the hands of its enemies. Law had lost all influence in the Council of Finance, and the company, being despoiled of its immunities, could no longer hold out the shadow of a prospect of being able to fulfil its engagements. All those suspected of illegal profits at the time the public delusion was at its height, were sought out and amerced in heavy fines. It was previously ordered that a list of the original proprietors should be made out, and that such persons as still retained their shares should place them in deposit with the company, and that those who had neglected to complete the shares for which they had put down their names should now purchase them of the company, at the rate of 13,500 livres for each share of 500 livres. Rather than submit to pay this enormous sum for stock which was actually at a discount, the shareholders packed up all their portable effects, and endeavoured to find a refuge in foreign countries. Orders were immediately issued to the authorities at the ports and frontiers, to apprehend all travellers who sought to leave the kingdom, and keep them in custody, until it was ascertained whether they had any plate or jewellery with them, or were concerned in the late stock-jobbing. Against such few as escaped, the punishment of death was recorded, while the most arbitrary proceedings were instituted against those who remained.

Law himself, in a moment of despair, determined to leave a country where his life was no longer secure. He at first only demanded permission to retire from Paris to one of his country-seats—a permission which the regent cheerfully granted. The latter was much affected at the unhappily turn affairs had taken, but his faith continued unmoved in the truth and efficacy of Law's financial system. His eyes were opened to his own errors; and during the few remaining years of his life he constantly longed for an opportunity of again establishing the system upon a securer basis. At Law's last interview with the prince, he is reported to have said,—"I confess that I have committed many faults. I committed them because I am a man, and all men are liable to error; but I declare to you most solemnly that none of them proceeded from wicked or dishonest motives, and that nothing of the kind will be found in the whole course of my conduct."

Two or three days after his departure the regent sent him a very kind letter, permitting him to leave the kingdom whenever he pleased, and stating that he had ordered his passports to be made ready. He at the same time offered him any sum of money he might require. Law respectfully declined the money, and set out for Brussels in a post-chaise belonging to Madame de Prie, the mistress of the Duke of Bourbon, escorted by six horse-guards. From thence he proceeded to Venice, where he remained for some months, the object of the greatest curiosity to the people, who believed him to be the possessor of enormous wealth. No opinion, however, could be more erroneous. With more generosity than could have been expected from a man who during the greatest part of his life had been a professed gambler, he had refused to enrich himself at the expense of a ruined nation. During the height of the popular frenzy for Mississippi stock, he had never doubted of the final success of his projects in making France the richest and most powerful nation of Europe. He invested all his gains in the purchase of landed property in France—a sure proof of his own belief in the stability of his schemes. He had hoarded no plate or jewellery, and sent no money, like the dishonest jobbers, to foreign countries. His all, with the exception of one diamond, worth about five or six thousand pounds sterling, was invested in the French soil; and when he left that country, he left it almost a beggar. This fact alone ought to rescue his memory from the charge of knavery, so often and so unjustly brought against him.

As soon as his departure was known, all his estates and his valuable library were confiscated. Among the rest, an annuity of 200,000 livres (8000*l*. sterling) on the lives of his wife and children, which had been purchased for five millions of livres, was forfeited, notwithstanding that a special edict, drawn up for the purpose in the days of his prosperity, had expressly declared that it should never be confiscated for any cause whatever. Great discontent existed among the people that Law had been suffered to escape. The mob and the parliament would have been pleased to have seen him hanged. The few who had not suffered by the commercial revolution rejoiced that the *quack* had left the country; but all those (and they were by far the most numerous class) whose fortunes were implicated regretted that his intimate knowledge of the distress of the country, and of the causes that had led to it, had not been rendered more available in discovering a remedy.

At a meeting of the Council of Finance and the General Council of the Regency, documents were laid upon the table,

from which it appeared that the amount of notes in circulation was 2700 millions. The regent was called upon to explain how it happened that there was a discrepancy between the dates at which these issues were made and those of the edicts by which they were authorised. He might have safely taken the whole blame upon himself, but he preferred that an absent man should bear a share of it; and he therefore stated that Law, upon his own authority, had issued 1200 millions of notes at different times, and that he (the regent), seeing that the thing had been irrevocably done, had screened Law by antedating the decrees of the council which authorised the augmentation. It would have been more to his credit if he had told the whole truth while he was about it, and acknowledged that it was mainly through his extravagance and impatience that Law had been induced to overstep the bounds of safe speculation. It was also ascertained that the national debt, on the 1st of January, 1721, amounted to upwards of 3100 millions of livres, or more than 124,000,000*l*. sterling, the interest upon which was 3,196,000*l*. A commission, or *visa,* was forthwith appointed to examine into all the securities of the state creditors, who were to be divided into five classes; the first four comprising those who had purchased their securities with real effects, and the latter comprising those who could give no proofs that the transactions they had entered into were real and *bonâ fide.* The securities of the latter were ordered to be destroyed, while those of the first four classes were subjected to a most rigid and jealous scrutiny. The result of the labours of the *visa* was a report, in which they counselled the reduction of the interest upon these securities to fifty-six millions of livres. They justified this advice by a statement of the various acts of peculation and extortion which they had discovered; and an edict to that effect was accordingly published and duly registered by the parliaments of the kingdom.

Another tribunal was afterwards established under the title of the *Chambre de l'Arsenal,* which took cognisance of all the malversations committed in the financial departments of the government during the late unhappy period. A Master of Requests, named Falhonet, together with the Abbé Clement, and two clerks in their employ, had been concerned in divers acts of peculation to the amount of upwards of a million of livres. The first two were sentenced to be beheaded, and the latter to be hanged; but their punishment was afterwards commuted into imprisonment for life in the Bastille. Numerous other acts of dishonesty were discovered, and punished by fine and imprisonment.

D'Argenson shared with Law and the regent the unpopularity which had alighted upon all those concerned in the Mississippi madness. He was dismissed from his post of Chancellor to make room for D'Aguesseau; but he retained the title of Keeper of Seals, and was allowed to attend the councils whenever he pleased. He thought it better, however, to withdraw from Paris, and live for a time a life of seclusion at his country seat. But he was not formed for retirement; and becoming moody and discontented, he aggravated a disease under which he had long laboured, and died in less than a twelve-month. The populace of Paris so detested him, that they carried their hatred even to his grave. As his funeral procession passed to the church of St. Nicholas du Chardonneret, the burying-place of his family, it was beset by a riotous mob; and his two sons, who were following as chief mourners, were obliged to drive as fast as they were able down a by-street to escape personal violence.

As regards Law, he for some time entertained a hope that he should be recalled to France to aid in establishing its credit upon a firmer basis. The death of the regent in 1723, who expired suddenly as he was sitting by the fireside conversing with his mistress, the Duchess de Phalaris, deprived him of that hope, and he was reduced to lead his former life of gambling. He was more than once obliged to pawn his diamond, the sole remnant of his vast wealth, but successful play generally enabled him to redeem it. Being persecuted by his creditors at Rome, he proceeded to Copenhagen, where he received permission from the English ministry to reside in his native country, his pardon for the murder of Mr. Wilson having been sent over to him in 1719. He was brought over in the admiral's ship—a circumstance which gave occasion for a short debate in the House of Lords. Earl Coningsby complained that a man who had renounced both his country and his religion should have been treated with such honour, and expressed his belief that his presence in England, at a time when the people were so bewildered by the nefarious practices of the South-Sea directors, would be attended with no little danger. He gave notice of a motion on the subject; but it was allowed to drop, no other member of the House having the slightest participation in his lordship's fears. Law remained for about four years in England, and then proceeded to Venice, where he died in 1729, in very embarrassed circumstances. The following epitaph was written at the time:

> "Ci gît cet Ecossais célébre,
> Ce calculateur sans égal,
> Qui, par les régles de l'algébre,
> A mis la France à l'hôpital."

His brother, William Law, who had been concerned with him in the administration both of the bank and the Louisiana Company, was imprisoned in the Bastille for alleged malversation, but no guilt was ever proved against him. He was liberated after fifteen months, and became the founder of a family, which is still known in France under the title of Marquises of Lauriston.

In the next chapter will be found an account of the madness which infected the people of England at the same time, and under very similar circumstances, but which, thanks to the energies and good sense of a constitutional government, was attended with results far less disastrous than those which were seen in France.

THE SOUTH-SEA BUBBLE

At length corruption, like a general flood,
Did deluge all; and avarice creeping on,
Spread, like a low-born mist, and hid the sun.
Statesmen and patriots plied alike the stocks,
Peeress and butler shared alike the box;
And judges jobbed, and bishops bit the town,
And mighty dukes packed cards for half-a-crown:
Britain was sunk in lucre's sordid charms.—*Pope.*

The South-Sea Company was originated by the celebrated Harley Earl of Oxford, in the year 1711, with the view of restoring public credit, which had suffered by the dismissal of the Whig ministry, and of providing for the discharge of the army and navy debentures, and other parts of the floating debt, amounting to nearly ten millions sterling. A company of merchants, at that time without a name, took this debt upon themselves, and the government agreed to secure them for a certain period the interest of six per cent. To provide for this interest, amounting to 600,000*l.* per annum, the duties upon wines, vinegar, India goods, wrought silks, tobacco, whale-fins, and some other articles, were rendered permanent. The monopoly of the trade to the South Seas was granted, and the company, being incorporated by act of parliament, assumed the title by which it has ever since been known. The minister took great credit to himself for his share in this transaction, and the scheme was always called by his flatterers "the Earl of Oxford's masterpiece."

Even at this early period of its history the most visionary ideas were formed by the company and the public of the immense riches of the eastern coast of South America. Every body had heard of the gold and silver mines of Peru and Mexico; every one believed them to be inexhaustible, and that it was only necessary to send the manufactures of England to the coast to be repaid a hundredfold in gold and silver ingots by the natives. A report industriously spread, that Spain was willing to concede four ports on the coasts of Chili and Peru for the purposes of traffic, increased the general confidence, and for many years the South-Sea Company's stock was in high favour.

Philip V. of Spain, however, never had any intention of admitting the English to a free trade in the ports of Spanish America. Negotiations were set on foot, but their only result was the *assiento* contract, or the privilege of supplying the colonies with negroes for thirty years, and of sending once a year a vessel, limited both as to tonnage and value of cargo, to trade with Mexico, Peru, or Chili. The latter permission was only granted upon the hard condition, that the King of Spain should enjoy one-fourth of the profits, and a tax of five per cent on the remainder. This was a great disappointment to the Earl of Oxford and his party, who were reminded much oftener than they found agreeable of the

"Parturiunt montes, nascitur ridiculus mus."

But the public confidence in the South-Sea Company was not shaken. The Earl of Oxford declared that Spain would permit two ships, in addition to the annual ship, to carry out merchandise during the first year; and a list was published, in which all the ports and harbours of these coasts were pompously set forth as open to the trade of Great Britain. The first voyage of the annual ship was not made till the year 1717, and in the following year the trade was suppressed by the rupture with Spain.

The king's speech, at the opening of the session of 1717, made pointed allusion to the state of public credit, and recommended that proper measures should be taken to reduce the national debt. The two great monetary corporations, the South-Sea Company and the Bank of England, made proposals to parliament on the 20th of May ensuing. The South-Sea Company prayed that their capital stock of ten millions might be increased to twelve, by subscription or otherwise, and offered to accept five per cent instead of six upon the whole amount. The bank made proposals equally advantageous. The house debated for some time, and finally three acts were passed, called the South-Sea Act, the Bank Act, and the General Fund Act. By the first, the proposals of the South-Sea Company were accepted, and that body held itself ready to advance the sum of two millions towards discharging the principal and interest of the debt due by the state for the four lottery funds of the ninth and tenth years of Queen Anne. By the second act, the bank received a lower rate of interest for the sum of 1,775,027*l.* 15*s.* due to it by the state, and agreed to deliver up to be cancelled as many exchequer bills as amounted to two millions sterling, and to accept of an annuity of one hundred thousand pounds, being after the rate of five per cent, the whole redeemable at one year's notice. They were further required to be ready to advance, in case of need, a sum not exceeding 2,500,000*l.* upon the same terms of five per cent interest, redeemable by parliament. The General Fund Act recited the various deficiencies, which were to be made good by the aids derived from the foregoing sources.

The name of the South-Sea Company was thus continually before the public. Though their trade with the South American States produced little or no augmentation of their revenues, they continued to flourish as a monetary corporation. Their stock was in high request, and the directors, buoyed up with success, began to think of new means for extending their influence. The Mississippi scheme of John Law, which so dazzled and captivated the French people, inspired them with an idea that they could carry on the same game in England. The anticipated failure of his plans did not divert them from their intention. Wise in their own conceit, they imagined they could avoid his faults, carry on their schemes for ever, and stretch the cord of credit to its extremest tension, without causing it to snap asunder.

It was while Law's plan was at its greatest height of popularity, while people were crowding in thousands to the Rue Quincampoix, and ruining themselves with frantic eagerness, that the South-Sea directors laid before parliament their famous plan for paying off the national debt. Visions of boundless wealth floated before the fascinated eyes of the people in the two most celebrated countries of Europe. The English commenced their career of extravagance somewhat later than the French; but as soon as the delirium seized them, they were determined not to be outdone. Upon the 22d of January, 1720, the House of Commons resolved itself into a committee of the whole house, to take into consideration that part of the king's speech at the opening of the session which related to the public debts, and the proposal of the South-Sea Company towards the redemption and sinking of the same. The proposal set forth at great length, and under several heads, the debts of the state, amounting to 30,981,712*l.*, which the company were anxious to take upon themselves, upon consideration of five per cent per annum, secured to them until Midsummer 1727; after which time, the whole was to become redeemable at the pleasure of the legislature, and the interest to be reduced to four per cent. The proposal was received with great favour; but the Bank of England had many friends in the House of Commons, who were desirous that that body should share in the advantages that were likely to accrue. On behalf of this corporation it was represented, that they had performed great and eminent services to the state in the most difficult times, and deserved, at least, that if any advantage was to be made by public bargains of this nature, they should be preferred before a company that had never done any thing for the nation. The further consideration of the matter was accordingly postponed for five days. In the mean time a plan was drawn up by the governors of the bank. The South-Sea Company, afraid that the bank might offer still more advantageous terms to the government than themselves, reconsidered their former proposal, and made some alterations in it, which they hoped would render it more acceptable. The principal change was a stipulation that the government might redeem these debts at the expiration of four years, instead of seven, as at first suggested. The bank resolved not to be outbidden in this singular auction, and the governors also reconsidered their first proposal, and sent in a new one.

Thus, each corporation having made two proposals, the house began to deliberate. Mr. Robert Walpole was the chief speaker in favour of the bank, and Mr. Aislabie, the Chancellor of the Exchequer, the principal advocate on behalf of the South-Sea Company. It was resolved, on the 2d of February, that the proposals of the latter were most advantageous to the country. They were accordingly received, and leave was given to bring in a bill to that effect.

Exchange Alley was in a fever of excitement. The company's stock, which had been at a hundred and thirty the previous day, gradually rose to three hundred, and continued to rise with the most astonishing rapidity during the whole time that the bill in its several stages was under discussion. Mr. Walpole was almost the only statesman in the House who spoke out boldly against it. He warned them, in eloquent and solemn language, of the evils that would ensue. It countenanced, he said, "the dangerous practice of stock-jobbing, and would divert the genius of the nation from trade and industry. It would hold out a dangerous lure to decoy the unwary to their ruin, by making them part with the earnings of their labour for a prospect of imaginary wealth. The great principle of the project was an evil of first-rate magnitude; it was to raise artificially the value of the stock, by exciting and keeping up a general infatuation, and by promising dividends out of funds which could never be adequate to the purpose." In a prophetic spirit he added, that if the plan succeeded, the directors would become masters of the government, form a new and absolute aristocracy in the kingdom, and control the resolutions of the legislature. If it failed, which he was convinced it would, the result would bring general discontent and ruin upon the country. Such would be the delusion, that when the evil day came, as come it would, the people would start up, as from a dream, and ask themselves if these things could have been true. All his eloquence was in vain. He was looked upon as a false prophet, or compared to the hoarse raven, croaking omens of evil. His friends, however, compared him to Cassandra, predicting evils which would only be believed when they come home to men's hearths, and stared them in the face at their own boards. Although, in former times, the House had listened with the utmost attention to every word that fell from his lips, the benches became deserted when it was known that he would speak on the South-Sea question.

The bill was two months in its progress through the House of Commons. During this time every exertion was made by the directors and their friends, and more especially by the chairman, the noted Sir John Blunt, to raise the price of the stock. The most extravagant rumours were in circulation. Treaties between England and Spain were spoken of, whereby the latter was to grant a free trade to all her colonies; and the rich produce of the mines of Potosi-la-Paz was to be brought to England until silver should become almost as plentiful as iron. For cotton and woollen goods, with which we could supply them in abundance, the dwellers in Mexico were to empty their golden mines. The company of merchants trading to the South Seas would be the richest the world ever saw, and every hundred pounds invested in it would produce hundreds per annum to the stockholder. At last the stock was raised by these means to near four hundred; but, after fluctuating a good deal, settled at three hundred and thirty, at which price it remained when the bill passed the Commons by a majority of 172 against 55.

In the House of Lords the bill was hurried through all its stages with unexampled rapidity. On the 4th of April it was read a first time; on the 5th, it was read a second time; on the 6th, it was committed; and on the 7th, was read a third time and passed.

Several peers spoke warmly against the scheme; but their warnings fell upon dull, cold ears. A speculating frenzy had seized them as well as the plebeians. Lord North and Grey said the bill was unjust in its nature, and might prove fatal in its consequences, being calculated to enrich the few and impoverish the many. The Duke of Wharton followed; but, as he only retailed at second-hand the arguments so eloquently stated by Walpole in the Lower House, he was not listened to with even the same attention that had been bestowed upon Lord North and Grey. Earl Cowper followed on the same side, and compared the bill to the famous horse of the siege of Troy. Like that, it was ushered in and received with great pomp and acclamations of joy, but bore within it treachery and destruction. The Earl of Sunderland endeavoured to answer all objections; and on the question being put, there appeared only seventeen peers against, and eighty-three in favour of the project. The very same day on which it passed the Lords, it received the royal assent, and became the law of the land.

It seemed at that time as if the whole nation had turned stock-jobbers. Exchange Alley was every day blocked up by crowds, and Cornhill was impassable for the number of carriages. Every body came to purchase stock. "Every fool aspired to be a knave." In the words of a ballad published at the time, and sung about the streets,*

> "Then stars and garters did appear
> Among the meaner rabble;
> To buy and sell, to see and hear
> The Jews and Gentiles squabble.
>
> The greatest ladies thither came,
> And plied in chariots daily,
> Or pawned their jewels for a sum
> To venture in the Alley."

The inordinate thirst of gain that had afflicted all ranks of society was not to be slaked even in the South Sea. Other schemes, of the most extravagant kind, were started. The share-lists were speedily filled up, and an enormous traffic carried on in shares, while, of course, every means were resorted to to raise them to an artificial value in the market.

Contrary to all expectations, South-Sea stock fell when the bill received the royal assent. On the 7th of April the shares were quoted at three hundred and ten, and on the following

---

* *A South-Sea Ballad; or, Merry Remarks upon Exchange-Alley Bubbles. To a new Tune called "The Grand Elixir; or, the Philosopher's Stone discovered."*

day at two hundred and ninety. Already the directors had tasted the profits of their scheme, and it was not likely that they should quietly allow the stock to find its natural level without an effort to raise it. Immediately their busy emissaries were set to work. Every person interested in the success of the project endeavoured to draw a knot of listeners around him, to whom he expatiated on the treasures of the South American seas. Exchange Alley was crowded with attentive groups. One rumour alone, asserted with the utmost confidence, had an immediate effect upon the stock. It was said that Earl Stanhope had received overtures in France from the Spanish government to exchange Gibraltar and Port Mahon for some places on the coast of Peru, for the security and enlargement of the trade in the South Seas. Instead of one annual ship trading to those ports, and allowing the king of Spain twenty-five per cent out of the profits, the company might build and charter as many ships as they pleased, and pay no per centage whatever to any foreign potentate.

"Visions of ingots danced before their eyes,"

and stock rose rapidly. On the 12th of April, five days after the bill had become law, the directors opened their books for a subscription of a million, at the rate of 300*l*. for every 100*l*. capital. Such was the concourse of persons of all ranks, that this first subscription was found to amount to above two millions of original stock. It was to be paid at five payments, of 60*l*. each for every 100*l*. In a few days the stock advanced to three hundred and forty, and the subscriptions were sold for double the price of the first payment. To raise the stock still higher, it was declared, in a general court of directors, on the 21st of April, that the midsummer dividend should be ten per cent, and that all subscriptions should be entitled to the same. These resolutions answering the end designed, the directors, to improve the infatuation of the monied men, opened their books for a second subscription of a million, at four hundred per cent. Such was the frantic eagerness of people of every class to speculate in these funds, that in the course of a few hours no less than a million and a half was subscribed at that rate.

In the mean time, innumerable joint-stock companies started up every where. They soon received the name of Bubbles, the most appropriate that imagination could devise. The populace are often most happy in the nicknames they employ. None could be more apt than that of Bubbles. Some of them lasted for a week or a fortnight, and were no more heard of, while others could not even live out that short span of existence. Every evening produced new schemes, and every morning new projects. The highest of the aristocracy were as eager in this hot pursuit of gain as the most plodding jobber in Cornhill. The Prince of Wales became governor of one company, and is said to have cleared 40,000*l.* by his speculations.* The Duke of Bridgewater started a scheme for the improvement of London and Westminster, and the Duke of Chandos another. There were nearly a hundred different projects, each more extravagant and deceptive than the other. To use the words of the *Political State,* they were "set on foot and promoted by crafty knaves, then pursued by multitudes of covetous fools, and at last appeared to be, in effect, what their vulgar appellation denoted them to be—bubbles and mere cheats." It was computed that near one million and a half sterling was won and lost by these unwarrantable practices, to the impoverishment of many a fool, and the enriching of many a rogue.

Some of these schemes were plausible enough, and, had they been undertaken at a time when the public mind was unexcited, might have been pursued with advantage to all concerned. But they were established merely with the view of raising the shares in the market. The projectors took the first opportunity of a rise to sell out, and next morning the scheme was at an end. Maitland, in his *History of London,* gravely informs us, that one of the projects which received great encouragement, was for the establishment of a company "to make deal

---

*Coxe's *Walpole,* Correspondence between Mr. Secretary Craggs and Earl Stanhope.

boards out of saw-dust." This is no doubt intended as a joke; but there is abundance of evidence to shew that dozens of schemes, hardly a whit more reasonable, lived their little day, ruining hundreds ere they fell. One of them was for a wheel for perpetual motion—capital one million; another was "for encouraging the breed of horses in England, and improving of glebe and church lands, and repairing and rebuilding parsonage and vicarage houses." Why the clergy, who were so mainly interested in the latter clause, should have taken so much interest in the first, is only to be explained on the supposition that the scheme was projected by a knot of the fox-hunting parsons, once so common in England. The shares of this company were rapidly subscribed for. But the most absurd and preposterous of all, and which shewed, more completely than any other, the utter madness of the people, was one started by an unknown adventurer, entitled, *"A company for carrying on an undertaking of great advantage, but nobody to know what it is."* Were not the fact stated by scores of credible witnesses, it would be impossible to believe that any person could have been duped by such a project. The man of genius who essayed this bold and successful inroad upon public credulity, merely stated in his prospectus that the required capital was half a million, in five thousand shares of 100*l.* each, deposit 2*l.* per share. Each subscriber, paying his deposit, would be entitled to 100*l.* per annum per share. How this immense profit was to be obtained, he did not condescend to inform them at that time, but promised that in a month full particulars should be duly announced, and a call made for the remaining 98*l.* of the subscription. Next morning, at nine o'clock, this great man opened an office in Cornhill. Crowds of people beset his door, and when he shut up at three o'clock, he found that no less than one thousand shares had been subscribed for, and the deposits paid. He was thus, in five hours, the winner of 2000*l.* He was philosopher enough to be contented with his venture, and set off the same evening for the Continent. He was never heard of again.

Well might Swift exclaim, comparing Change Alley to a gulf in the South Sea:

"Subscribers here by thousands float,
　　And jostle one another down,
Each paddling in his leaky boat,
　　And here they fish for gold and drown.

Now buried in the depths below,
　　Now mounted up to heaven again,
They reel and stagger to and fro,
　　At their wits' end, like drunken men.

Meantime, secure on Garraway cliffs,
　　A savage race, by shipwrecks fed,
Lie waiting for the foundered skiffs,
　　And strip the bodies of the dead."

Another fraud that was very successful was that of the "Globe *Permits*," as they were called. They were nothing more than square pieces of playing-cards, on which was the impression of a seal, in wax, bearing the sign of the Globe Tavern, in the neighbourhood of Exchange Alley, with the inscription of "Sail-Cloth Permits." The possessors enjoyed no other advantage from them than permission to subscribe at some future time to a new sail-cloth manufactory, projected by one who was then known to be a man of fortune, but who was afterwards involved in the peculation and punishment of the South-Sea directors. These permits sold for as much as sixty guineas in the Alley.

Persons of distinction, of both sexes, were deeply engaged in all these bubbles; those of the male sex going to taverns and coffee-houses to meet their brokers, and the ladies resorting for the same purpose to the shops of milliners and haberdashers. But it did not follow that all these people believed in the feasibility of the schemes to which they subscribed; it was enough for their purpose that their shares would, by stock-jobbing arts, be soon raised to a premium, when they got rid of them with all expedition to the really credulous. So great was the confusion of the crowd in the alley, that shares in the same bubble were known to have been sold at the same instant ten per cent higher at one end of the alley than at the other. Sensible men beheld the extraordinary infatuation of the people with sorrow and alarm. There were some both in and out of parliament who foresaw clearly the ruin that was impending. Mr. Walpole did not cease his gloomy forebodings. His fears were shared by all the thinking few, and impressed most forcibly upon the government. On the 11th of June, the day the parliament rose, the king published a proclamation, declaring that all these unlawful projects should be deemed public nuisances, and prosecuted accordingly, and forbidding any broker, under a penalty of five hundred pounds, from buying or selling any shares in them. Notwithstanding this proclamation, roguish speculators still carried them on, and the deluded people still encouraged them. On the 12th of July, an order of the Lords Justices assembled in privy council was published, dismissing all the petitions that had been presented for patents and charters, and dissolving all the bubble companies. The following copy of their lordships' order, containing a list of all these nefarious projects, will not be deemed uninteresting at the present time, when, at periodic intervals, there is but too much tendency in the public mind to indulge in similar practices:

"At the Council Chamber, Whitehall, the 12th day of July, 1720. Present, their Excellencies the Lords Justices in Council.

"Their Excellencies the Lords Justices, in council, taking into consideration the many inconveniences arising to the public from several projects set on foot for raising of joint-stock for various purposes, and that a great many of his majesty's subjects have been drawn in to part with their money on pretence of assurances that their petitions for patents and charters to enable them to carry on the same would be granted: to prevent such impositions, their excellencies this day ordered the said several petitions, together with such reports from the Board of Trade, and from his majesty's attorney and solicitor-general, as had been obtained thereon, to be laid before them; and after mature consideration thereof, were pleased, by advice of his majesty's privy council, to order that the said petitions be dismissed, which are as follow:

"1. Petition of several persons, praying letters patent for carrying on a fishing trade by the name of the Grand Fishery of Great Britain.

"2. Petition of the Company of the Royal Fishery of England, praying letters patent for such further powers as will effectually contribute to carry on the said fishery.

"Petition of George James, on behalf of himself and divers persons of distinction concerned in a national fishery, praying letters patent of incorporation, to enable them to carry on the same.

"4. Petition of several merchants, traders, and others, whose names are thereunto subscribed, praying to be incorporated for reviving and carrying on a whale fishery to Greenland and elsewhere.

"5. Petition of Sir John Lambert and others thereto subscribing, on behalf of themselves and a great number of merchants, praying to be incorporated for carrying on a Greenland trade, and particularly a whale fishery in Davis's Straits.

"6. Another petition for a Greenland trade.

"7. Petition of several merchants, gentlemen, and citizens, praying to be incorporated for buying and building of ships to let or freight.

"8. Petition of Samuel Antrim and others, praying for letters patent for sowing hemp and flax.

"9. Petition of several merchants, masters of ships, sailmakers, and manufacturers of sail-cloth, praying a charter of incorporation, to enable them to carry on and promote the said manufactory by a joint-stock.

"10. Petition of Thomas Boyd and several hundred merchants, owners and masters of ships, sail-makers, weavers, and other traders, praying a charter of incorporation, empowering them to borrow money for purchasing lands, in order to the manufacturing sail-cloth and fine holland.

"11. Petition on behalf of several persons interested in a patent granted by the late King William and Queen Mary for the making of linen and sail-cloth, praying that no charter may be granted to any persons whatsoever for making sail-cloth, but that the privilege now enjoyed by them may be confirmed, and likewise an additional power to carry on the cotton and cotton-silk manufactures.

"12. Petition of several citizens, merchants, and traders in London, and others, subscribers to a British stock for a general insurance from fire in any part of England, praying to be incorporated for carrying on the said undertaking.

"13. Petition of several of his majesty's loyal subjects of the city of London and other parts of Great Britain, praying to be incorporated for carrying on a general insurance from losses by fire within the kingdom of England.

"14. Petition of Thomas Burges and others his majesty's subjects thereto subscribing, in behalf of themselves and others, subscribers to a fund of 1,200,000l. for carrying on a trade to his majesty's German dominions, praying to be incorporated by the name of the Harburg Company.

"15. Petition of Edward Jones, a dealer in timber, on behalf of himself and others, praying to be incorporated for the importation of timber from Germany.

"16. Petition of several merchants of London, praying a charter of incorporation for carrying on a salt-work.

"17. Petition of Captain Macphedris of London, merchant, on behalf of himself and several merchants, clothiers, hatters, dyers, and other traders, praying a charter of incorporation empowering them to raise a sufficient sum of money to purchase lands for planting and rearing a wood called madder, for the use of dyers.

"18. Petition of Joseph Galendo of London, snuff-maker, praying a patent for his invention to prepare and cure Virginia tobacco for snuff in Virginia, and making it into the same in all his majesty's dominions."

List of Bubbles

The following Bubble-Companies were by the same order declared to be illegal, and abolished accordingly:

1. For the importation of Swedish iron.
2. For supplying London with sea-coal. Capital, three millions.
3. For building and rebuilding houses throughout all England. Capital, three millions.
4. For making of muslin.
5. For carrying on and improving the British alum-works.
6. For effectually settling the island of Blanco and Sal Tartagus.
7. For supplying the town of Deal with fresh water.
8. For the importation of Flanders lace.
9. For improvement of lands in Great Britain. Capital, four millions.
10. For encouraging the breed of horses in England, and improving of glebe and church lands, and for repairing and rebuilding parsonage and vicarage houses.
11. For making of iron and steel in Great Britain.
12. For improving the land in the county of Flint. Capital, one million.
13. For purchasing lands to build on. Capital, two millions.
14. For trading in hair.
15. For erecting salt-works in Holy Island. Capital, two millions.
16. For buying and selling estates, and lending money on mortgage.
17. For carrying on an undertaking of great advantage; but nobody to know what it is.
18. For paving the streets of London. Capital, two millions.

19. For furnishing funerals to any part of Great Britain.

20. For buying and selling lands and lending money at interest. Capital, five millions.

21. For carrying on the royal fishery of Great Britain. Capital, ten millions.

22. For assuring of seamen's wages.

23. For erecting loan-offices for the assistance and encouragement of the industrious. Capital, two millions.

24. For purchasing and improving leaseable lands. Capital, four millions.

25. For importing pitch and tar, and other naval stores, from North Britain and America.

26. For the clothing, felt, and pantile trade.

27. For purchasing and improving a manor and royalty in Essex.

28. For insuring of horses. Capital, two millions.

29. For exporting the woollen manufacture, and importing copper, brass, and iron. Capital, four millions.

30. For a grand dispensary. Capital, three millions.

31. For erecting mills and purchasing lead-mines. Capital, two millions.

32. For improving the art of making soap.

33. For a settlement on the island of Santa Cruz.

34. For sinking pits and smelting lead ore in Derbyshire.

35. For making glass bottles and other glass.

36. For a wheel for perpetual motion. Capital, one million.

37. For improving of gardens.

38. For insuring and increasing children's fortunes.

39. For entering and loading goods at the Custom-house, and for negotiating business for merchants.

40. For carrying on a woollen manufacture in the north of England.

41. For importing walnut-trees from Virginia. Capital, two millions.

42. For making Manchester stuffs of thread and cotton.

43. For making Joppa and Castile soap.

44. For improving the wrought-iron and steel manufactures of this kingdom. Capital, four millions.

45. For dealing in lace, hollands, cambrics, lawns, &c. Capital, two millions.

46. For trading in and improving certain commodities of the produce of this kingdom, &c. Capital, three millions.

47. For supplying the London markets with cattle.

48. For making looking-glasses, coach-glasses, &c. Capital, two millions.

49. For working the tin and lead mines in Cornwall and Derbyshire.

50. For making rape-oil.

51. For importing beaver fur. Capital, two millions.

52. For making pasteboard and packing-paper.

53. For importing of oils and other materials used in the woollen manufacture.

54. For improving and increasing the silk manufactures.

55. For lending money on stock, annuities, tallies, &c.

56. For paying pensions to widows and others, at a small discount. Capital, two millions.

57. For improving malt liquors. Capital, four millions.

58. For a grand American fishery.

59. For purchasing and improving the fenny lands in Lincolnshire. Capital, two millions.

60. For improving the paper manufacture of Great Britain.

61. The Bottomry Company.

62. For drying malt by hot air.

63. For carrying on a trade in the river Oronooko.

64. For the more effectual making of baize, in Colchester and other parts of Great Britain.

65. For buying of naval stores, supplying the victualling, and paying the wages of the workmen.

66. For employing poor artificers, and furnishing merchants and others with watches.

67. For improvement of tillage and the breed of cattle.

68. Another for the improvement of our breed in horses.

69. Another for a horse-insurance.

70. For carrying on the corn trade of Great Britain.

71. For insuring to all masters and mistresses the losses they may sustain by servants. Capital, three millions.

72. For erecting houses or hospitals for taking in and maintaining illegitimate children. Capital, two millions.

73. For bleaching coarse sugars, without the use of fire or loss of substance.

74. For building turnpikes and wharfs in Great Britain.

75. For insuring from thefts and robberies.

76. For extracting silver from lead.

77. For making china and delft ware. Capital, one million.

78. For importing tobacco, and exporting it again to Sweden and the north of Europe. Capital, four millions.

79. For making iron with pit coal.

80. For furnishing the cities of London and Westminster with hay and straw. Capital, three millions.

81. For a sail and packing-cloth manufactory in Ireland.

82. For taking up ballast.

83. For buying and fitting out ships to suppress pirates.

84. For the importation of timber from Wales. Capital, two millions.

85. For rock-salt.

86. For the transmutation of quicksilver into a malleable fine metal.

Besides these bubbles, many others sprang up daily, in spite of the condemnation of the government and the ridicule of the still sane portion of the public. The print-shops teemed with caricatures, and the newspapers with epigrams and satires, upon the prevalent folly. An ingenious cardmaker published a pack of South-Sea playing-cards, which are now extremely rare, each card containing, besides the usual figures of a very small size, in one corner, a caricature of a bubble company, with appropriate verses underneath. One of the most famous bubbles was "Puckle's Machine Company," for discharging round and square cannon-balls and bullets, and making a total revolution in the art of war. Its pretensions to public favour were thus summed up on the eight of spades:

> "A rare invention to destroy the crowd
> Of fools at home instead of fools abroad.
> Fear not, my friends, this terrible machine,
> They're only wounded who have shares therein."

The nine of hearts was a caricature of the English Copper and Brass Company, with the following epigram:

> "The headlong fool that wants to be a swopper
> Of gold and silver coin for English copper,
> May, in Change Alley, prove himself an ass,
> And give rich metal for adultrate brass."

The eight of diamonds celebrated the company for the colonisation of Acadia, with this doggrel:

> "He that is rich and wants to fool away
> A good round sum in North America,
> Let him subscribe himself a headlong sharer,
> And asses' ears shall honour him or bearer."

And in a similar style every card of the pack exposed some knavish scheme, and ridiculed the persons who were its dupes. It was computed that the total amount of the sums proposed for carrying on these projects was upwards of three hundred millions sterling.

It is time, however, to return to the great South-Sea gulf, that swallowed the fortunes of so many thousands of the avaricious and the credulous. On the 29th of May, the stock had risen as high as five hundred, and about two-thirds of the government annuitants had exchanged the securities of the state for those of the South-Sea company. During the whole of the month of May the stock continued to rise, and on the 28th it was quoted at five hundred and fifty. In four days after this it took a prodigious leap, rising suddenly from five hundred and fifty to eight hundred and ninety. It was now the general opinion that the stock could rise no higher, and many persons took that opportunity of selling out, with a view of realising their profits. Many noblemen and persons in the train of the king, and about to accompany him to Hanover, were also anxious to sell out. So many sellers, and so few buyers, appeared in the Alley on the 3d of June, that the stock fell at once from eight hundred and ninety to six hundred and forty. The directors were alarmed, and gave their agents orders to buy. Their efforts succeeded. Towards evening, confidence was restored, and the stock advanced to seven hundred and fifty. It continued at this price, with some slight fluctuation, until the company closed their books on the 22d of June.

It would be needless and uninteresting to detail the various arts employed by the directors to keep up the price of stock. It will be sufficient to state that it finally rose to one thousand per cent. It was quoted at this price in the commencement of August. The bubble was then full-blown, and began to quiver and shake preparatory to its bursting.

Many of the government annuitants expressed dissatisfaction against the directors. They accused them of partiality in making out the lists for shares in each subscription. Further uneasiness was occasioned by its being generally known that

Sir John Blunt the chairman, and some others, had sold out. During the whole of the month of August the stock fell, and on the 2d of September it was quoted at seven hundred only.

The state of things now became alarming. To prevent, if possible, the utter extinction of public confidence in their proceedings, the directors summoned a general court of the whole corporation, to meet in Merchant Tailors' Hall on the 8th of September. By nine o'clock in the morning, the room was filled to suffocation; Cheapside was blocked up by a crowd unable to gain admittance, and the greatest excitement prevailed. The directors and their friends mustered in great numbers. Sir John Fellowes, the sub-governor, was called to the chair. He acquainted the assembly with the cause of their meeting; read to them the several resolutions of the court of directors, and gave them an account of their proceedings; of the taking in the redeemable and unredeemable funds, and of the subscriptions in money. Mr. Secretary Craggs then made a short speech, wherein he commended the conduct of the directors, and urged that nothing could more effectually contribute to the bringing this scheme to perfection than union among themselves. He concluded with a motion for thanking the court of directors for their prudent and skilful management, and for desiring them to proceed in such manner as they should think most proper for the interest and advantage of the corporation. Mr. Hungerford, who had rendered himself very conspicuous in the House of Commons for his zeal in behalf of the South-Sea company, and who was shrewdly suspected to have been a considerable gainer by knowing the right time to sell out, was very magniloquent on this occasion. He said that he had seen the rise and fall, the decay and resurrection of many communities of this nature, but that, in his opinion, none had ever performed such wonderful things in so short a time as the South-Sea company. They had done more than the crown, the pulpit, or the bench could do. They had reconciled all parties in one common interest; they had laid asleep, if not wholly extinguished, all the domestic jars and animosities of the nation. By the rise of their stock, monied men had vastly increased their fortunes; country gentlemen had seen the value of their lands doubled and trebled in their hands. They had at the same time done good to the Church, not a few of the reverend clergy having got great sums by the project. In short, they had enriched the whole nation, and he hoped they had not forgotten themselves. There was some hissing at the latter part of this speech, which for the extravagance of its eulogy was not far removed from satire; but the directors and their friends, and all the winners in the room, applauded vehemently. The Duke of Portland spoke in a similar strain, and expressed his great wonder why any body should be dissatisfied; of course, he was a winner by his speculations, and in a condition similar to that of the fat alderman in *Joe Miller's Jests,* who, whenever he had eaten a good dinner, folded his hands upon his paunch, and expressed his doubts whether there could be a hungry man in the world.

Several resolutions were passed at this meeting, but they had no effect upon the public. Upon the very same evening the stock fell to six hundred and forty, and on the morrow to five hundred and forty. Day after day it continued to fall, until it was as low as four hundred. In a letter dated September 13th, from Mr. Broderick, M.P., to Lord Chancellor Middleton, and published in Coxe's *Walpole,* the former says: "Various are the conjectures why the South-Sea directors have suffered the cloud to break so early. I made no doubt but they would do so when they found it to their advantage. They have stretched credit so far beyond what it would bear, that specie proves insufficient to support it. Their most considerable men have drawn out, securing themselves by the losses of the deluded, thoughtless numbers, whose understandings have been overruled by avarice and the hope of making mountains out of mole-hills. Thousands of families will be reduced to beggary. The consternation is inexpressible—the rage beyond description, and the case altogether so desperate, that I do not see any plan or scheme so much as thought of for averting the blow; so that I cannot pretend to guess what is next to be done." Ten days afterwards, the stock still falling, he writes: "The company have yet come to no determination, for they are in such a wood that they know not which way to turn. By several gentlemen lately come to town, I perceive the very name of a South-Sea-man grows abominable in every country. A great many goldsmiths are already run off, and more will daily. I question whether one-third, nay, one-fourth of them can stand it. From the very beginning, I founded my judgment of the whole affair upon the unquestionable maxim, that ten millions (which is more than our running cash) could not circulate two hundred millions beyond which our paper credit extended. That, therefore, whenever that should become doubtful, be the cause what it would, our noble state machine must inevitably fall to the ground."

On the 12th of September, at the earnest solicitation of Mr. Secretary Craggs, several conferences were held between the directors of the South Sea and the directors of the Bank. A report which was circulated, that the latter had agreed to circulate six millions of the South-Sea company's bonds, caused the stock to rise to six hundred and seventy; but in the afternoon, as soon as the report was known to be groundless, the stock fell again to five hundred and eighty; the next day to five hundred and seventy, and so gradually to four hundred.*

The ministry were seriously alarmed at the aspect of affairs. The directors could not appear in the streets without being insulted; dangerous riots were every moment apprehended. Despatches were sent off to the king at Hanover, praying his immediate return. Mr. Walpole, who was staying at his country seat, was sent for, that he might employ his known influence with the directors of the Bank of England to induce them to accept the proposal made by the South-Sea company for circulating a number of their bonds.

---

*Gay (the poet), in that disastrous year, had a present from young Craggs of some South-Sea stock, and once supposed himself to be master of twenty thousand pounds. His friends persuaded him to sell his share, but he dreamed of dignity and splendour, and could not bear to obstruct his own fortune. He was then importuned to sell as much as would purchase a hundred a year for life, "which," says Fenton, "will make you sure of a clean shirt and a shoulder of mutton every day." This counsel was rejected; the profit and principal were lost, and Gay sunk under the calamity so low that his life became in danger.—*Johnson's Lives of the Poets.*

The Bank was very unwilling to mix itself up with the affairs of the company; it dreaded being involved in calamities which it could not relieve, and received all overtures with visible reluctance. But the universal voice of the nation called upon it to come to the rescue. Every person of note in commercial politics was called in to advise in the emergency. A rough draft of a contract drawn up by Mr. Walpole was ultimately adopted as the basis of further negotiations, and the public alarm abated a little.

On the following day, the 20th of September, a general court of the South-Sea company was held at Merchant Tailors' Hall, in which resolutions were carried, empowering the directors to agree with the Bank of England, or any other persons, to circulate the company's bonds, or make any other agreement with the Bank which they should think proper. One of the speakers, a Mr. Pulteney, said it was most surprising to see the extraordinary panic which had seized upon the people. Men were running to and fro in alarm and terror, their imaginations filled with some great calamity, the form and dimensions of which nobody knew:

> "Black it stood as night—
> Fierce as ten furies—terrible as hell."

At a general court of the Bank of England, held two days afterwards, the governor informed them of the several meetings that had been held on the affairs of the South-Sea company, adding that the directors had not yet thought fit to come to any decision upon the matter. A resolution was then proposed, and carried without a dissentient voice, empowering the directors to agree with those of the South-Sea to circulate their bonds, to what sum, and upon what terms, and for what time, they might think proper.

Thus both parties were at liberty to act as they might judge best for the public interest. Books were opened at the Bank for a subscription of three millions for the support of public credit, on the usual terms of 15*l.* per cent deposit, 3*l.* per cent premium, and 5*l.* per cent interest. So great was the concourse of people in the early part of the morning, all eagerly bringing their money, that it was thought the subscription would be filled that day; but before noon the tide turned. In spite of all that could be done to prevent it, the South-Sea company's stock fell rapidly. Their bonds were in such discredit, that a run commenced upon the most eminent goldsmiths and bankers, some of whom, having lent out great sums upon South-Sea stock, were obliged to shut up their shops and abscond. The Sword-blade company, who had hitherto been the chief cashiers of the South-Sea company, stopped payment. This being looked upon as but the beginning of evil, occasioned a great run upon the bank, who were now obliged to pay out money much faster than they had received it upon the subscription in the morning. The day succeeding was a holiday (the 29th of September), and the Bank had a little breathing time. They bore up against the storm; but their former rivals, the South-Sea company, were wrecked upon it. Their stock fell to one hundred and fifty, and gradually, after various fluctuations, to one hundred and thirty-five.

The Bank finding they were not able to restore public confidence, and stem the tide of ruin, without running the risk of being swept away with those they intended to save, declined to carry out the agreement into which they had partially entered. They were under no obligation whatever to continue; for the so-called Bank contract was nothing more than the rough draft of an agreement, in which blanks had been left for several important particulars, and which contained no penalty for their secession. "And thus," to use the words of the Parliamentary History, "were seen, in the space of eight months, the rise, progress, and fall of that mighty fabric, which, being wound up by mysterious springs to a wonderful height, had fixed the eyes and expectations of all Europe, but whose foundation, being fraud, illusion, credulity, and infatuation, fell to the ground as soon as the artful management of its directors was discovered."

In the hey-day of its blood, during the progress of this dangerous delusion, the manners of the nation became sensibly corrupted. The parliamentary inquiry, set on foot to discover the delinquents, disclosed scenes of infamy, disgraceful alike to the morals of the offenders and the intellects of the people among whom they had arisen. It is a deeply interesting study to investigate all the evils that were the result. Nations, like individuals, cannot become desperate gamblers with impunity. Punishment is sure to overtake them sooner or later. A celebrated writer* is quite wrong when he says "that such an era as this is the most unfavourable for a historian; that no reader of sentiment and imagination can be entertained or interested by a detail of transactions such as these, which admit of no warmth, no colouring, no embellishment; a detail of which only serves to exhibit an inanimate picture of tasteless vice and mean degeneracy." On the contrary,—and Smollett might have discovered it, if he had been in the humour,—the subject is capable of inspiring as much interest as even a novelist can desire. Is there no warmth in the despair of a plundered people?—no life and animation in the picture which might be drawn of the woes of hundreds of impoverished and ruined families? of the wealthy of yesterday become the beggars of today? of the powerful and influential changed into exiles and outcasts, and the voice of self-reproach and imprecation resounding from every corner of the land? Is it a dull or uninstructive picture to see a whole people shaking suddenly off the trammels of reason, and running wild after a golden vision, refusing obstinately to believe that it is not real, till, like a deluded hind running after an *ignis fatuus,* they are plunged into a quagmire? But in this false spirit has history too often been written. The intrigues of unworthy courtiers to gain the favour of still more unworthy kings, or the records of murderous battles and sieges, have been dilated on, and told over and over again, with all the eloquence of style and all the charms of fancy; while the circumstances which have most deeply affected the morals and welfare of the people have been passed over with but slight notice, as dry and dull, and capable of neither warmth nor colouring.

---

* Smollett.

During the progress of this famous bubble, England pre-sented a singular spectacle. The public mind was in a state of unwholesome fermentation. Men were no longer satisfied with the slow but sure profits of cautious industry. The hope of boundless wealth for the morrow made them heedless and ex-travagant for to-day. A luxury, till then unheard of, was intro-duced, bringing in its train a corresponding laxity of morals. The overbearing insolence of ignorant men, who had arisen to sudden wealth by successful gambling, made men of true gen-tility of mind and manners blush that gold should have power to raise the unworthy in the scale of society. The haughtiness of some of these "cyphering cits," as they were termed by Sir Richard Steele, was remembered against them in the day of their adversity. In the parliamentary inquiry, many of the di-rectors suffered more for their insolence than for their pecula-tion. One of them, who, in the full-blown pride of an ignorant rich man, had said that he would feed his horse upon gold, was reduced almost to bread and water for himself; every haughty look, every overbearing speech, was set down, and repaid them a hundredfold in poverty and humiliation.

The state of matters all over the country was so alarming, that George I. shortened his intended stay in Hanover, and re-turned in all haste to England. He arrived on the 11th of Novem-ber, and parliament was summoned to meet on the 8th of December. In the mean time, public meetings were held in every considerable town of the empire, at which petitions were adopted, praying the vengeance of the legislature upon the South-Sea directors, who, by their fraudulent practices, had brought the nation to the brink of ruin. Nobody seemed to imag-ine that the nation itself was as culpable as the South-Sea company. Nobody blamed the credulity and avarice of the people—the degrading lust of gain, which had swallowed up every nobler quality in the national character, or the infatuation which had made the multitude run their heads with such frantic eagerness into the net held out for them by scheming projectors. These things were never mentioned. The people were a simple, honest, hard-working people, ruined by a gang of robbers, who were to be hanged, drawn, and quartered without mercy.

This was the almost unanimous feeling of the country. The two Houses of Parliament were not more reasonable. Before the guilt of the South-Sea directors was known, punishment was the only cry. The king, in his speech from the throne, expressed his hope that they would remember that all their prudence, temper, and resolution were necessary to find out and apply the proper remedy for their misfortunes. In the debate on the answer to the address, several speakers indulged in the most violent invectives against the directors of the South-Sea project. The Lord Molesworth was particularly vehement.

"It had been said by some, that there was no law to punish the directors of the South-Sea company, who were justly looked upon as the authors of the present misfortunes of the state. In his opinion, they ought upon this occasion to follow the example of the ancient Romans, who, having no law against parricide, because their legislators supposed no son could be so unnaturally wicked as to embrue his hands in his father's blood, made a law to punish this heinous crime as soon as it was committed. They adjudged the guilty wretch to be sewn in a sack, and thrown alive into the Tiber. He looked upon the contrivers and executors of the villanous South-Sea scheme as the parricides of their country, and should be satisfied to see them tied in like manner in sacks, and thrown into the Thames." Other members spoke with as much want of temper and discretion. Mr. Walpole was more moderate. He recommended that their first care should be to restore public credit. "If the city of London were on fire, all wise men would aid in extinguishing the flames, and preventing the spread of the conflagration, before they inquired after the incendiaries. Public credit had received a dangerous wound, and lay bleeding, and they ought to apply a speedy remedy to it. It was time enough to punish the assassin afterwards." On the 9th of December, an address, in answer to his majesty's speech, was agreed upon, after an amendment, which was carried without a division, that words should be added expressive of the determination of the House not only to seek a remedy for the national distresses, but to punish the authors of them.

The inquiry proceeded rapidly. The directors were ordered to lay before the House a full account of all their proceedings. Resolutions were passed to the effect that the calamity was mainly owing to the vile arts of stock-jobbers, and that nothing could tend more to the re-establishment of public credit than a law to prevent this infamous practice. Mr. Walpole then rose, and said, that "as he had previously hinted, he had spent some time upon a scheme for restoring public credit, but that the execution of it depending upon a position which had been laid down as fundamental, he thought it proper, before he opened out his scheme, to be informed whether he might rely upon that foundation. It was, whether the subscription of public debts and encumbrances, money subscriptions, and other contracts, made with the South-Sea company, should remain in the present state?" This question occasioned an animated debate. It was finally agreed, by a majority of 259 against 117, that all these contracts should remain in their present state, unless altered for the relief of the proprietors by a general court of the South-Sea company, or set aside by due course of law. On the following day, Mr. Walpole laid before a committee of the whole house his scheme for the restoration of public credit, which was, in substance, to engraft nine millions of South-Sea Stock into the Bank of England, and the same sum into the East India company upon certain conditions. The plan was favourably received by the House. After some few objections, it was ordered that proposals should be received from the two great corporations. They were both unwilling to lend their aid, and the plan met with a warm but fruitless opposition at the general courts summoned for the purpose of deliberating upon it. They, however, ultimately agreed upon the terms on which they would consent to circulate the South-Sea bonds, and their report being presented to the committee, a bill was brought in under the superintendence of Mr. Walpole, and safely carried through both Houses of Parliament.

A bill was at the same time brought in for restraining the South-Sea directors, governor, sub-governor, treasurer, cashier, and clerks from leaving the kingdom for a twelvemonth, and for discovering their estates and effects, and preventing them from transporting or alienating the same. All the most influential members of the House supported the bill. Mr. Shippen, seeing Mr. Secretary Craggs in his place, and believing the injurious rumours that were afloat of that minister's conduct in the South-Sea business, determined to touch him to the quick. He said he was glad to see a British House of Commons resuming its pristine vigour and spirit, and acting with so much unanimity for the public good. It was necessary to secure the persons and estates of the South-Sea directors and their officers; "but," he added, looking fixedly at Mr. Craggs as he spoke, "there were other men in high station, whom, in time, he would not be afraid to name, who were no less guilty than the directors." Mr. Craggs arose in great wrath, and said, that if the inuendo were directed against him, he was ready to give satisfaction to any man who questioned him, either in the House or out of it. Loud cries of order immediately arose on every side. In the midst of the uproar, Lord Molesworth got up, and expressed his wonder at the boldness of Mr. Craggs in challenging the whole House of Commons. He, Lord Molesworth, though somewhat old, past sixty, would answer Mr. Craggs whatever he had to say in the House, and he trusted there were plenty of young men beside him, who would not be afraid to look Mr. Craggs in the face out of the House. The cries of order again resounded from every side; the members arose simultaneously; everybody seemed to be vociferating at once. The Speaker in vain called order. The confusion lasted several minutes, during which Lord Molesworth and Mr. Craggs were almost the only members who kept their seats. At last, the call for Mr. Craggs became so violent, that he thought proper to submit to the universal feeling of the House, and explain his unparliamentary expression. He said, that by giving satisfaction to the impugners of his conduct in that House, he did not mean that he would fight, but that he would explain his conduct. Here the matter ended, and the House proceeded to debate in what manner they should conduct their inquiry into the affairs of the South-Sea company, whether in a grand or a select committee. Ultimately, a secret committee of thirteen was appointed, with power to send for persons, papers, and records.

The Lords were as zealous and as hasty as the Commons. The Bishop of Rochester said the scheme had been like a pestilence. The Duke of Wharton said the House ought to shew no respect of persons; that, for his part, he would give up the dearest friend he had, if he had been engaged in the project. The nation had been plundered in a most shameful and flagrant manner, and he would go as far as anybody in the punishment of the offenders. Lord Stanhope said, that every farthing possessed by the criminals, whether directors or not directors, ought to be confiscated, to make good the public losses.

During all this time the public excitement was extreme. We learn from Coxe's *Walpole,* that the very name of a South-Sea director was thought to be synonymous with every species of fraud and villany. Petitions from counties, cities, and boroughs, in all parts of the kingdom, were presented, crying for the justice due to an injured nation and the punishment of the villanous peculators. Those moderate men, who would not go to extreme lengths, even in the punishment of the guilty, were accused of being accomplices, were exposed to repeated insults and virulent invectives, and devoted, both in anonymous letters and public writings, to the speedy vengeance of an injured people. The accusations against Mr. Aislabie, Chancellor of the Exchequer, and Mr. Craggs, another member of the ministry, were so loud, that the House of Lords resolved to proceed at once into the investigation concerning them. It was ordered, on the 21st of January, that all brokers concerned in the South-Sea scheme should lay before the House an account of the stock or subscriptions bought or sold by them for any of the officers of the Treasury or Exchequer, or in trust for any of them, since Michaelmas 1719. When this account was delivered, it appeared that large quantities of stock had been transferred to the use of Mr. Aislabie. Five of the South-Sea directors, including Mr. Edward Gibbon, the grandfather of the celebrated historian, were ordered into the custody of the black rod. Upon a motion made by Earl Stanhope, it was unanimously resolved, that the taking in or giving credit for stock without a valuable consideration actually paid or sufficiently secured; or the purchasing stock by any director or agent of the South-Sea company, for the use or benefit of any member of the administration, or any member of either House of Parliament, during such time as the South-Sea bill was yet pending in Parliament, was a notorious and dangerous corruption. Another resolution was passed a few days afterwards, to the effect that several of the directors and officers of the company having, in a clandestine manner, sold their own stock to the company, had been guilty of a notorious fraud and breach of trust, and had thereby mainly caused the unhappy turn of affairs that had so much affected public credit. Mr. Aislabie resigned his office as Chancellor of the Exchequer, and absented himself from parliament, until the formal inquiry into his individual guilt was brought under the consideration of the legislature.

In the mean time, Knight, the treasurer of the company, and who was entrusted with all the dangerous secrets of the dishonest directors, packed up his books and documents and made his escape from the country. He embarked in disguise, in a small boat on the river, and proceeding to a vessel hired for the purpose, was safely conveyed to Calais. The Committee of Secrecy informed the House of the circumstance, when it was resolved unanimously that two addresses should be presented to the king; the first praying that he would issue a proclamation offering a reward for the apprehension of Knight; and the second, that he would give immediate orders to stop the ports, and to take effectual care of the coasts, to prevent the said Knight, or any other officers of the South-Sea company, from escaping out of the kingdom. The ink was hardly dry upon these addresses before they were carried to the king by Mr. Methuen, deputed by the House for that purpose. The same evening a royal proclamation was issued, offering a reward of two thousand pounds for the apprehension of Knight. The Commons ordered the doors of the House to be locked, and the keys to be placed on the table. General Ross, one of the members of the Committee of Secrecy, acquainted them that they had already discovered a train of the deepest villany and fraud that hell had ever contrived to ruin a nation, which in due time they would lay before the House. In the mean time, in order to a further discovery, the Committee thought it highly necessary to secure the persons of some of the directors and principal South-Sea officers, and to seize their papers. A motion to this effect having been made, was carried unanimously. Sir Robert Chaplin, Sir Theodore Janssen, Mr. Sawbridge, and Mr. F. Eyles, members of the House, and directors of the South-Sea company, were summoned to appear in their places, and answer for their corrupt practices. Sir Theodore Janssen and Mr. Sawbridge answered to their names, and endeavoured to exculpate themselves. The House heard them patiently, and then ordered them to withdraw. A motion was then made, and carried *nemine contradicente,* that they had been guilty of a notorious breach of trust—had occasioned much loss to great numbers of his majesty's subjects, and had highly prejudiced the public credit. It was then ordered that, for their offence, they should be expelled the House, and taken into custody of the sergeant-at-arms. Sir Robert Chaplin and Mr. Eyles, attending in their places four days afterwards, were also expelled the House. It was resolved at the same time to address the king to give directions to his ministers at foreign courts to make application for Knight, that he might be delivered up to the English authorities, in case he took refuge in any of their dominions. The king at once agreed, and messengers were despatched to all parts of the continent the same night.

Among the directors taken into custody was Sir John Blunt, the man whom popular opinion has generally accused of having been the original author and father of the scheme. This man, we are informed by Pope, in his epistle to Allen Lord Bathurst, was a Dissenter, of a most religious deportment, and professed to be a great believer.

> "'God cannot love,' says Blunt, with tearless eyes,
> 'The wretch he starves,' and piously denies. . . . .
> Much-injur'd Blunt! why bears he Britain's hate?
> A wizard told him in these words our fate:
> 'At length corruption, like a general flood,
> So long by watchful ministers withstood,
> Shall deluge all; and avarice, creeping on,

Spread like a low-born mist, and blot the sun;
Statesman and patriot ply alike the stocks,
Peeress and butler share alike the box,
And judges job, and bishops bite the town,
And mighty dukes pack cards for half-a-crown:
See Britain sunk in Lucre's sordid charms
And France revenged on Anne's and Edward's arms!'
'Twas no court-badge, great Scrivener! fir'd thy brain,
Nor lordly luxury, nor city gain:
No, 'twas thy righteous end, asham'd to see
Senates degen'rate, patriots disagree,
And nobly wishing party-rage to cease,
To buy both sides, and give thy country peace."
Pope's Epistle to Allen Lord Bathurst.

He constantly declaimed against the luxury and corruption of the age, the partiality of parliaments, and the misery of party-spirit. He was particularly eloquent against avarice in great and noble persons. He was originally a scrivener, and afterwards became not only a director, but the most active manager of the South-Sea company. Whether it was during his career in this capacity that he first began to declaim against the avarice of the great, we are not informed. He certainly must have seen enough of it to justify his severest anathema; but if the preacher had himself been free from the vice he condemned, his declamations would have had a better effect. He was brought up in custody to the bar of the House of Lords, and underwent a long examination. He refused to answer several important questions. He said he had been examined already by a committee of the House of Commons, and as he did not remember his answers, and might contradict himself, he refused to answer before another tribunal. This declaration, in itself an indirect proof of guilt, occasioned some commotion in the House. He was again asked peremptorily whether he had ever sold any portion of the stock to any member of the administration, or any member of either House of Parliament, to facilitate the passing of the bill. He again declined to answer. He was anxious, he said, to treat the House with all possible respect, but he thought it hard to be compelled to accuse himself. After several ineffectual attempts to refresh his memory, he was directed to withdraw. A violent discussion ensued between the friends and opponents of the ministry. It was asserted that the administration were no strangers to the convenient taciturnity of Sir John Blunt. The Duke of Wharton made a reflection upon the Earl Stanhope, which the latter warmly resented. He spoke under great excitement, and with such vehemence as to cause a sudden determination of blood to the head. He felt himself so ill that he was obliged to leave the House and retire to his chamber. He was cupped immediately, and also let blood on the following morning, but with slight relief. The fatal result was not anticipated. Towards evening he became drowsy, and turning himself on his face, expired. The sudden death of this statesman caused great grief to the nation. George I. was exceedingly affected, and shut himself up for some hours in his closet, inconsolable for his loss.

Knight, the treasurer of the company, was apprehended at Tirlemont, near Liege, by one of the secretaries of Mr. Leathes, the British resident at Brussels, and lodged in the citadel of Antwerp. Repeated applications were made to the court of Austria to deliver him up, but in vain. Knight threw himself upon the protection of the states of Brabant, and demanded to be tried in that country. It was a privilege granted to the states of Brabant by one of the articles of the *Joyeuse Entrée,* that every criminal apprehended in that country should be tried in that country. The states insisted on their privilege, and refused to deliver Knight to the British authorities. The latter did not cease their solicitations; but in the mean time, Knight escaped from the citadel.

On the 16th of February the Committee of Secrecy made their first report to the House. They stated that their inquiry had been attended with numerous difficulties and embarrassments; every one they had examined had endeavoured, as far as in him lay, to defeat the ends of justice. In some of the books produced before them, false and fictitious entries had been made; in others, there were entries of money with blanks for the name of the stockholders. There were frequent erasures and alterations, and in some of the books leaves were torn out. They also found that some books of great importance had been destroyed altogether, and that some had been taken away or secreted. At the very entrance into their inquiry, they had observed that the matters referred to them were of great variety and extent. Many persons had been entrusted with various parts in the execution of the law, and under colour thereof had acted in an unwarrantable manner, in disposing of the properties of many thousands of persons amounting to many millions of money. They discovered that, before the South-Sea Act was passed, there was an entry in the company's books of the sum of 1,259,325*l.*, upon account of stock stated to have been sold to the amount of 574,500*l.* This stock was all fictitious, and had been disposed of with a view to promote the passing of the bill. It was noted as sold on various days, and at various prices, from 150 to 325 percent. Being surprised to see so large an account disposed of at a time when the company were not empowered to increase their capital, the Committee determined to investigate most carefully the whole transaction. The governor, sub-governor, and several directors were brought before them, and examined rigidly. They found that, at the time these entries were made, the company was not in possession of such a quantity of stock, having in their own right only a small quantity, not exceeding thirty thousand pounds at the utmost. Pursuing the inquiry, they found that this amount of stock was to be esteemed as taken in or holden by the company for the benefit of the pretended purchasers, although no mutual agreement was made for its delivery or acceptance at any certain time. No money was paid down, nor any deposit or security whatever given to the company by the supposed purchasers; so that if the stock had fallen, as might have been expected had the act not passed, they would have sustained no loss. If, on the contrary, the price of stock advanced (as it actually did by the success of the scheme), the difference by the advanced price was to be made good to them. Accordingly, after the passing of the act, the account of stock was made up and adjusted with Mr. Knight, and the pretended purchasers were paid the difference out of the company's cash. This fictitious stock, which had been chiefly at the disposal of Sir John Blunt, Mr. Gibbon, and Mr. Knight, was distributed among several members of the government and their connexions, by way of bribe, to facilitate the passing of the bill. To the Earl of Sunderland was assigned 50,000*l.* of this stock; to the Duchess of Kendal, 10,000*l.*; to the Countess of Platen, 10,000*l.*; to her two nieces, 10,000*l.*; to Mr. Secretary Craggs, 30,000*l.*; to Mr. Charles Stanhope (one of the secretaries of the Treasury), 10,000*l.*; to the Sword-blade company, 50,000*l.* It also appeared that Mr. Stanhope had received the enormous sum of 250,000*l.* as the difference in the price of some stock, through the hands of Turner, Caswall, and Co., but that his name had been partly erased from their books, and altered to Stangape. Aislabie, the Chancellor of the Exchequer, had made profits still more abominable. He had an account with the same firm, who were also South-Sea directors, to the amount of 794,451*l.* He had, besides, advised the company to make their second subscription one million and a half, instead of a million, by their own authority, and without any warrant. The third subscription had been conducted in a manner as disgraceful. Mr. Aislabie's name was down for 70,000*l.*; Mr. Craggs, senior, for 659,000*l.*; the Earl of Sunderland's for 160,000*l.*; and Mr. Stanhope for 47,000*l.* This report was succeeded by six others, less important. At the end of the last, the committee declared, that the absence of Knight, who had been principally entrusted, prevented them from carrying on their inquiries.

The first report was ordered to be printed, and taken into consideration on the next day but one succeeding. After a very angry and animated debate, a series of resolutions were agreed to, condemnatory of the conduct of the directors, of the members of the parliament and of the administration concerned with them; and declaring that they ought, each and all, to make satisfaction out of their own estates for the injury they had done the public. Their practices were declared to be corrupt, infamous, and dangerous; and a bill was ordered to be brought in for the relief of the unhappy sufferers.

Mr. Charles Stanhope was the first person brought to account for his share in these transactions. He urged in his defence that, for some years past, he had lodged all the money he was possessed of in Mr. Knight's hands, and whatever stock

Mr. Knight had taken in for him, he had paid a valuable consideration for it. As for the stock that had been bought for him by Turner, Caswall, and Co., he knew nothing about it. Whatever had been done in that matter was done without his authority, and he could not be responsible for it. Turner and Co. took the latter charge upon themselves; but it was notorious to every unbiassed and unprejudiced person that Mr. Stanhope was a gainer of the 250,000*l.* which lay in the hands of that firm to his credit. He was, however, acquitted by a majority of three only. The greatest exertions were made to screen him. Lord Stanhope, the son of the Earl of Chesterfield, went round to the wavering members, using all the eloquence he was possessed of to induce them either to vote for the acquittal, or to absent themselves from the House. Many weak-headed country gentlemen were led astray by his persuasions, and the result was as already stated. The acquittal caused the greatest discontent throughout the country. Mobs of a menacing character assembled in different parts of London; fears of riots were generally entertained, especially as the examination of a still greater delinquent was expected by many to have a similar termination. Mr. Aislabie, whose high office and deep responsibilities should have kept him honest, even had native principle been insufficient, was very justly regarded as perhaps the greatest criminal of all. His case was entered into on the day succeeding the acquittal of Mr. Stanhope. Great excitement prevailed, and the lobbies and avenues of the House were beset by crowds impatient to know the result. The debate lasted the whole day. Mr. Aislabie found few friends: his guilt was so apparent and so heinous that nobody had courage to stand up in his favour. It was finally resolved, without a dissentient voice, that Mr. Aislabie had encouraged and promoted the destructive execution of the South-Sea scheme with a view to his own exorbitant profit, and had combined with the directors in their pernicious practices, to the ruin of the public trade and credit of the kingdom: that he should for his offences be ignominiously expelled from the House of Commons, and committed a close prisoner to the Tower of London; that he should be restrained from going out of the kingdom for a whole year, or till the end of the next session of parliament; and that he should make out a correct account of all his estate, in order that it might be applied to the relief of those who had suffered by his mal-practices.

This verdict caused the greatest joy. Though it was delivered at half-past twelve at night, it soon spread over the city. Several persons illuminated their houses in token of their joy. On the following day, when Mr. Aislabie was conveyed to the Tower, the mob assembled on Tower-hill with the intention of hooting and pelting him. Not succeeding in this, they kindled a large bonfire, and danced around it in the exuberance of their delight. Several bonfires were made in other places; London presented the appearance of a holiday, and people congratulated one another as if they had just escaped from some great calamity. The rage upon the acquittal of Mr. Stanhope had grown to such a height, that none could tell where it would have ended, had Mr. Aislabie met with the like indulgence.

To increase the public satisfaction, Sir George Caswall, of the firm of Turner, Caswall, and Co., was expelled from the House on the following day, committed to the Tower, and ordered to refund the sum of 250,000*l*.

That part of the report of the Committee of Secrecy which related to the Earl of Sunderland was next taken into consideration. Every effort was made to clear his lordship from the imputation. As the case against him rested chiefly on the evidence extorted from Sir John Blunt, great pains were taken to make it appear that Sir John's word was not to be believed, especially in a matter affecting the honour of a peer and privy councillor. All the friends of the ministry rallied around the earl, it being generally reported that a verdict of guilty against him would bring a Tory ministry into power. He was eventually acquitted by a majority of 233 against 172; but the country was convinced of his guilt. The greatest indignation was everywhere expressed, and menacing mobs again assembled in London. Happily no disturbance took place.

This was the day on which Mr. Craggs the elder expired. The morrow had been appointed for the consideration of his case. It was very generally believed that he had poisoned himself. It appeared, however, that grief for the loss of his son, one of the secretaries of the Treasury, who had died five weeks previously of the small-pox, preyed much on his mind. For this son, dearly beloved, he had been amassing vast heaps of riches: he had been getting money, but not honestly; and he for whose sake he had bartered his honour and sullied his fame was now no more. The dread of further exposure increased his trouble of mind, and ultimately brought on an apoplectic fit, in which he expired. He left a fortune of a million and a half, which was afterwards confiscated for the benefit of the sufferers by the unhappy delusion he had been so mainly instrumental in raising.

One by one the case of every director of the company was taken into consideration. A sum amounting to two millions and fourteen thousand pounds was confiscated from their estates towards repairing the mischief they had done, each man being allowed a certain residue in proportion to his conduct and circumstances, with which he might begin the world anew. Sir John Blunt was only allowed 5000*l.* out of his fortune of upwards of 183,000*l.*; Sir John Fellows was allowed 10,000*l.* out of 243,000*l.*; Sir Theodore Janssen, 50,000*l.* out of 243,000*l.*; Mr. Edward Gibbon, 10,000*l.* out of 106,000*l.*; Sir John Lambert, 5000*l.* out of 72,000*l.* Others, less deeply involved, were treated with greater liberality. Gibbon, the historian, whose grandfather was the Mr. Edward Gibbon so severely mulcted, has given, in the *Memoirs of his Life and Writings,* an interesting account of the proceedings in parliament at this time. He owns that he is not an unprejudiced witness; but, as all the writers from which it is possible to extract any notice of the proceedings of these disastrous years were prejudiced on the other side, the statements of the great historian become of additional value. If only on the principle of *audi alteram partem,* his opinion is entitled to consideration. "In the year 1716," he says, "my grandfather was elected one of the directors of the South-Sea company, and his books exhibited the proof that before his acceptance of that fatal office, he had acquired an independent fortune of 60,000*l.* But his fortune was overwhelmed in the shipwreck of the year 1720, and the labours of thirty years were blasted in a single day. Of the use or abuse of the South-Sea scheme, of the guilt or innocence of my grandfather and his brother directors, I am neither a competent nor a disinterested judge. Yet the equity of modern times must condemn the violent and arbitrary proceedings, which would have disgraced the cause of justice, and rendered injustice still more odious. No sooner had the nation awakened from its golden dream, than a popular and even a parliamentary clamour demanded its victims; but it was acknowledged on all sides, that the directors, however guilty, could not be touched by any known laws of the land. The intemperate notions of Lord Molesworth were not literally acted on; but a bill of pains and penalties was introduced—a retroactive statute, to punish the offences which did not exist at the time they were committed. The legislature restrained the persons of the directors, imposed an exorbitant security for their appearance, and marked their character with a previous note of ignominy. They were compelled to deliver, upon oath, the strict value of their estates, and were disabled from making any transfer or alienation of any part of their property. Against a bill of pains and penalties, it is the common right of every subject to be heard by his counsel at the bar. They prayed to be heard. Their prayer was refused, and their oppressors, who required no evidence, would listen to no defence. It had been at first proposed, that one-eighth of their respective estates should be allowed for the future support of the directors; but it was especially urged that, in the various shades of opulence and guilt, such a proportion would be too light for many, and for some might possibly be too heavy. The character and conduct of each man were separately weighed; but, instead of the calm solemnity of a judicial inquiry, the fortune and honour of thirty-three Englishmen were made the topics of hasty conversation, the sport of a lawless majority; and the basest member of the committee, by a malicious word or a silent vote, might indulge his general spleen or personal animosity. Injury was aggravated by insult, and insult was embittered by pleasantry. Allowances of 20*l.* or 1*s.* were facetiously moved. A vague report that a director had formerly been concerned in another project, by which some unknown persons had lost their money, was admitted as a proof of his actual guilt. One man was ruined because he had dropped a foolish speech, that his horses should feed upon gold; another, because he was grown so proud, that one day, at the Treasury, he had refused a civil answer to persons much above him. All were condemned, absent and unheard, in arbitrary fines and forfeitures, which swept away the greatest part of their substance. Such bold oppression can scarcely be shielded by the omnipotence of parliament. My grandfather could not expect to be treated with more lenity than his companions. His Tory principles and connexions rendered him obnoxious to the ruling powers. His name was reported in a suspicious secret. His well-known abilities could not plead the excuse of ignorance or error. In the first proceedings against the South-Sea directors, Mr. Gibbon was one of the first taken into custody, and in the final sentence the measure of his fine proclaimed him eminently guilty. The total estimate, which he delivered on oath to the House of Commons, amounted to 106,543*l.* 5*s.* 6*d.*, exclusive of antecedent settlements. Two different allowances of 15,000*l.* and of 10,000*l.* were moved for Mr. Gibbon; but on the question being put, it was carried without a division for the smaller sum. On these ruins, with the skill and credit of which parliament had not been able to despoil him, my grandfather, at a mature age, erected the edifice of a new fortune. The labours of sixteen years were amply rewarded; and I have reason to believe that the second structure was not much inferior to the first."

The next consideration of the legislature, after the punishment of the directors, was to restore public credit. The scheme of Walpole had been found insufficient, and had fallen into disrepute. A computation was made of the whole capital stock of the South-Sea company at the end of the year 1720. It was found to amount to thirty-seven millions eight hundred thousand pounds, of which the stock allotted to all the proprietors only amounted to twenty-four millions five hundred thousand pounds. The remainder of thirteen millions three hundred thousand pounds belonged to the company in their corporate capacity, and was the profit they had made by the national delusion. Upwards of eight millions of this were taken from the company, and divided among the proprietors and subscribers generally, making a dividend of about 33*l.* 6*s.* 8*d.* per cent. This was a great relief. It was further ordered, that such persons as had borrowed money from the South-Sea company upon stock actually transferred and pledged at the time of borrowing to or for the use of the company, should be free from all demands, upon payment of ten per cent of the sums so borrowed. They had lent about eleven millions in this manner, at a time when prices were unnaturally raised; and they now received back one million one hundred thousand, when prices had sunk to their ordinary level.

But it was a long time before public credit was thoroughly restored. Enterprise, like Icarus, had soared too high, and melted the wax of her wings; like Icarus, she had fallen into a sea, and learned, while floundering in its waves, that her proper element was the solid ground. She has never since attempted so high a flight.

In times of great commercial prosperity there has been a tendency to over-speculation on several occasions since then. The success of one project generally produces others of a similar kind. Popular imitativeness will always, in a trading nation, seize hold of such successes, and drag a community too anxious for profits into an abyss from which extrication is difficult. Bubble companies, of a kind similar to those engendered by the South-Sea project, lived their little day in the famous year of the panic, 1825. On that occasion, as in 1720, knavery gathered a rich harvest from cupidity, but both suffered when the day of reckoning came. The schemes of the year 1836 threatened, at one time, results as disastrous; but they were happily averted before it was too late.*

---

*The South-Sea project remained until 1845 the greatest example in British history of the infatuation of the people for commercial gambling. The first edition of these volumes was published some time before the outbreak of the Great Railway Mania of that and the following year.

THE TULIPOMANIA

Quis furor, ô cives!—*Lucan.*

The tulip—so named, it is said, from a Turkish word, signifying a turban—was introduced into western Europe about the middle of the sixteenth century. Conrad Gesner, who claims the merit of having brought it into repute,—little dreaming of the commotion it was shortly afterwards to make in the world,—says that he first saw it in the year 1559, in a garden at Augsburg, belonging to the learned Counsellor Herwart, a man very famous in his day for his collection of rare exotics. The bulbs were sent to this gentleman by a friend at Constantinople, where the flower had long been a favourite. In the course of ten or eleven years after this period, tulips were much sought after by the wealthy, especially in Holland and Germany. Rich people at Amsterdam sent for the bulbs direct to Constantinople, and paid the most extravagant prices for them. The first roots planted in England were brought from Vienna in 1600. Until the year 1634 the tulip annually increased in reputation, until it was deemed a proof of bad taste in any man of fortune to be without a collection of them. Many learned men, including Pompeius de Angelis, and the celebrated Lipsius of Leyden, the author of the treatise "De Constantia," were passionately fond of tulips. The rage for possessing them soon caught the middle classes of society, and merchants and shopkeepers, even of moderate means, began to vie with each other in the rarity of these flowers and the preposterous prices they paid for them. A trader at Harlaem was known to pay one-half of his fortune for a single root, not with the design of selling it again at a profit, but to keep in his own conservatory for the admiration of his acquaintance.

One would suppose that there must have been some great virtue in this flower to have made it so valuable in the eyes of so prudent a people as the Dutch; but it has neither the beauty nor the perfume of the rose—hardly the beauty of the "sweet, sweet-pea;" neither is it as enduring as either. Cowley, it is true, is loud in its praise. He says—

> "The tulip next appeared, all over gay,
> But wanton, full of pride, and full of play;
> The world can't show a dye but here has place;
> Nay, by new mixtures, she can change her face;
> Purple and gold are both beneath her care,
> The richest needlework she loves to wear;
> Her only study is to please the eye,
> And to outshine the rest in finery."

This, though not very poetical, is the description of a poet. Beckmann, in his *History of Inventions,* paints it with more fidelity, and in prose more pleasing than Cowley's poetry. He says, "There are few plants which acquire, through accident, weakness, or disease, so many variegations as the tulip. When uncultivated, and in its natural state, it is almost of one colour, has large leaves, and an extraordinarily long stem. When it has been weakened by cultivation, it becomes more agreeable in the eyes of the florist. The petals are then paler, smaller, and more diversified in hue; and the leaves acquire a softer green colour. Thus this masterpiece of culture, the more beautiful it turns, grows so much the weaker, so that, with the greatest skill and most careful attention, it can scarcely be transplanted, or even kept alive."

Many persons grow insensibly attached to that which gives them a great deal of trouble, as a mother often loves her sick and ever-ailing child better than her more healthy offspring. Upon the same principle we must account for the unmerited encomia lavished upon these fragile blossoms. In 1634, the rage among the Dutch to possess them was so great that the ordinary industry of the country was neglected, and the population, even to its lowest dregs, embarked in the tulip trade. As the mania increased, prices augmented, until, in the year 1635, many persons were known to invest a fortune of 100,000 florins in the purchase of forty roots. It then became necessary to sell them by their weight in *perits,* a small weight less than a grain. A tulip of the species called *Admiral Liefken,* weighing 400 *perits,* was worth 4400 florins; an *Admiral Van der Eyck,* weighing 446 *perits,* was worth 1260 florins; a *Childer* of 106 *perits* was worth 1615 florins; a *Viceroy* of 400 *perits,* 3000 florins; and, most precious of all, a *Semper Augustus,* weighing 200 *perits,* was thought to be very cheap at 5500 florins. The latter was much sought after, and even an inferior bulb might command a price of 2000 florins. It is related that, at one time, early in 1636, there were only two roots of this description to be had in all Holland, and those not of the best. One was in the possession of a dealer in Amsterdam, and the other in Harlaem. So anxious were the speculators to obtain them, that one person offered the fee-simple of twelve acres of building-ground for the Harlaem tulip. That of Amsterdam was bought for 4600 florins, a new carriage, two grey horses, and a complete set of harness. Munting, an industrious author of that day, who wrote a folio volume of one thousand pages upon the tulipomania, has preserved the following list of the various articles, and their value, which were delivered for one single root of the rare species called the *Viceroy:*

	florins
Two lasts of wheat.	448
Four lasts of rye	558
Four fat oxen.	480
Eight fat swine	240
Twelve fat sheep.	120
Two Hogsheads of wine	70
Four tuns of beer.	32
Two tuns of butter.	192
One thousand lbs. of cheese.	120
A complete bed	100
A suit of clothes	80
A silver drinking-cup	60
	2500

People who had been absent from Holland, and whose chance it was to return when this folly was at its maximum, were sometimes led into awkward dilemmas by their ignorance. There is an amusing instance of the kind related in Blainville's *Travels.* A wealthy merchant, who prided himself not a little on his rare tulips, received upon one occasion a very valuable consignment of merchandise from the Levant. Intelligence of its arrival was brought him by a sailor, who presented himself for that purpose at the counting-house, among bales of goods of every description. The merchant, to reward him for his news, munificently made him a present of a fine red herring for his breakfast. The sailor had, it appears, a great partiality for onions, and seeing a bulb very like an onion lying upon the counter of this liberal trader, and thinking it, no doubt, very much out of its place among silks and velvets, he slily seized an opportunity and slipped it into his pocket, as a relish for his herring. He got clear off with his prize, and proceeded to the quay to eat his breakfast. Hardly was his back turned when the merchant missed his valuable *Semper Augustus,* worth three thousand florins, or about 280*l.* sterling. The whole establishment was instantly in an uproar; search was everywhere made for the precious root, but it was not to be found. Great was the merchant's distress of mind. The search was renewed, but again without success. At last some one thought of the sailor.

The unhappy merchant sprang into the street at the bare suggestion. His alarmed household followed him. The sailor, simple soul! had not thought of concealment. He was found quietly sitting on a coil of ropes, masticating the last morsel of his *"onion."* Little did he dream that he had been eating a breakfast whose cost might have regaled a whole ship's crew for a twelvemonth; or, as the plundered merchant himself expressed it, "might have sumptuously feasted the Prince of Orange and the whole court of the Stadtholder." Anthony caused pearls to be dissolved in wine to drink the health of Cleopatra; Sir Richard Whittington was as foolishly magnificent in an entertainment to King Henry V.; and Sir Thomas Gresham drank a diamond dissolved in wine to the health of Queen Elizabeth, when she opened the Royal Exchange; but the breakfast of this roguish Dutchman was as splendid as either. He had an advantage, too, over his wasteful predecessors: *their* gems did not improve the taste or the wholesomeness of *their* wine, while *his* tulip was quite delicious with his red herring. The most unfortunate part of the business for him was, that he remained in prison for some months on a charge of felony preferred against him by the merchant.

Another story is told of an English traveller, which is scarcely less ludicrous. This gentleman, an amateur botanist, happened to see a tulip-root lying in the conservatory of a wealthy Dutchman. Being ignorant of its quality, he took out his penknife, and peeled off its coats, with the view of making experiments upon it. When it was by this means reduced to half its size, he cut it into two equal sections, making all the time many learned remarks on the singular appearances of the unknown bulb. Suddenly the owner pounced upon him, and, with fury in his eyes, asked him if he knew what he had been doing? "Peeling a most extraordinary onion," replied the philosopher. *"Hundert tausend duyvel!"* said the Dutchman; "it's an *Admiral Van der Eyck*." "Thank you," replied the traveller, taking out his note-book to make a memorandum of the same; "are these admirals common in your country?" "Death and the Devil!" said the Dutchman, seizing the astonished man of science by the collar; "come before the syndic, and you shall see." In spite of his remonstrances, the traveller was led through the streets followed by a mob of persons. When brought into the presence of the magistrate, he learned, to his consternation, that the root upon which he had been experimentalising was worth four thousand florins; and, notwithstanding all he could urge in extenuation, he was lodged in prison until he found securities for the payment of this sum.

The demand for tulips of a rare species increased so much in the year 1636, that regular marts for their sale were established on the Stock Exchange of Amsterdam, in Rotterdam, Harlaem, Leyden, Alkmar, Hoorn, and other towns. Symptoms of gambling now became, for the first time, apparent. The stock-jobbers, ever on the alert for a new speculation, dealt largely in tulips, making use of all the means they so well knew how to employ to cause fluctuations in prices. At first, as in all these gambling mania, confidence was at its height, and every body gained. The tulip-jobbers speculated in the rise and fall of the tulip stocks, and made large profits by buying when prices fell, and selling out when they rose. Many individuals grew suddenly rich. A golden bait hung temptingly out before the people, and one after the other, they rushed to the tulip-marts, like flies around a honey-pot. Every one imagined that the passion for tulips would last for ever, and that the wealthy from every part of the world would send to Holland, and pay whatever prices were asked for them. The riches of Europe would be concentrated on the shores of the Zuyder Zee, and poverty banished from the favoured clime of Holland. Nobles, citizens, farmers, mechanics, seamen, footmen, maid-servants, even chimney-sweeps and old clotheswomen, dabbled in tulips. People of all grades converted their property into cash, and invested it in flowers. Houses and lands were offered for sale at ruinously low prices, or assigned in payment of bargains made at the tulip-mart. Foreigners became smitten with the same frenzy, and money poured into Holland from all directions. The prices of the necessaries of life rose again by degrees: houses and lands, horses and carriages, and luxuries of every sort, rose in value with them, and for some months Holland seemed the very antechamber of Plutus. The operations of the trade became so extensive and so intricate, that it was found necessary to draw up a code of laws for the guidance of the dealers. Notaries and clerks were also appointed, who devoted themselves exclusively to the interests of the trade. The designation of public notary was hardly known in some towns, that of tulip-notary usurping its place. In the smaller towns, where there was no exchange, the principal tavern was usually selected as the "show-place," where high and low traded in tulips, and confirmed their bargains over sumptuous entertainments. These dinners were sometimes attended by two or three hundred persons, and large vases of tulips, in full bloom, were placed at regular intervals upon the tables and sideboards for their gratification during the repast.

At last, however, the more prudent began to see that this folly could not last for ever. Rich people no longer bought the flowers to keep them in their gardens, but to sell them again at cent per cent profit. It was seen that somebody must lose fearfully in the end. As this conviction spread, prices fell, and never rose again. Confidence was destroyed, and a universal panic seized upon the dealers. *A* had agreed to purchase ten *Semper Augustines* from *B,* at four thousand florins each, at six weeks after the signing of the contract. *B* was ready with the flowers at the appointed time; but the price had fallen to three or four hundred florins, and *A* refused either to pay the difference or receive the tulips. Defaulters were announced day after day in all the towns of Holland. Hundreds who, a few months previously, had begun to doubt that there was such a thing as poverty in the land suddenly found themselves the possessors of a few bulbs, which nobody would buy, even though they offered them at one quarter of the sums they had paid for them. The cry of distress resounded every where, and each man accused his neighbour. The few who had contrived to enrich themselves hid their wealth from the knowledge of their fellow-citizens, and invested it in the English or other funds. Many who, for a brief season, had emerged from the humbler walks of life, were cast back into their original obscurity. Substantial merchants were reduced almost to beggary, and many a representative of a noble line saw the fortunes of his house ruined beyond redemption.

When the first alarm subsided, the tulip-holders in the several towns held public meetings to devise what measures were best to be taken to restore public credit. It was generally agreed that deputies should be sent from all parts to Amsterdam, to consult with the government upon some remedy for the evil. The government at first refused to interfere, but advised the tulip-holders to agree to some plan among themselves. Several meetings were held for this purpose; but no measure could be devised likely to give satisfaction to the deluded people, or repair even a slight portion of the mischief that had been done. The language of complaint and reproach was in every body's mouth, and all the meetings were of the most stormy character. At last, however, after much bickering and ill-will, it was agreed, at Amsterdam, by the assembled deputies, that all contracts made in the height of the mania, or prior to the month of November, 1636, should be declared null and void, and that, in those made after that date, purchasers should be freed from their engagements, on paying ten per cent to the vendor. This decision gave no satisfaction. The vendors who had their tulips on hand were, of course, discontented, and those who had pledged themselves to purchase, thought themselves hardly treated. Tulips which had, at one time, been worth six thousand florins, were now to be procured for five hundred; so that the composition of ten per cent was one hundred florins more than the actual value. Actions for breach of contract were threatened in all the courts of the country; but the latter refused to take cognisance of gambling transactions.

The matter was finally referred to the Provincial Council at the Hague, and it was confidently expected that the wisdom of this body would invent some measure by which credit should be restored. Expectation was on the stretch for its decision, but it never came. The members continued to deliberate week after week, and at last, after thinking about it for three months, declared that they could offer no final decision until they had more information. They advised, however, that, in the meantime, every vendor should, in the presence of witnesses, offer the tulips *in natura* to the purchaser for the sums agreed upon. If the latter refused to take them, they might be put up for sale by public auction, and the original contractor held responsible for the difference between the actual and the stipulated price. This was exactly the plan recommended by the deputies, and which was already shown to be of no avail. There was no court in Holland which would enforce payment. The question was raised in Amsterdam, but the judges unanimously refused to interfere, on the ground that debts contracted in gambling were no debts in law.

Thus the matter rested. To find a remedy was beyond the power of the government. Those who were unlucky enough to have had stores of tulips on hand at the time of the sudden re-action were left to bear their ruin as philosophically as they could; those who had made profits were allowed to keep them; but the commerce of the country suffered a severe shock, from which it was many years ere it recovered.

The example of the Dutch was imitated to some extent in England. In the year 1636 tulips were publicly sold in the Ex-change of London, and the jobbers exerted themselves to the ut-most to raise them to the fictitious value they had acquired in Amsterdam. In Paris also the jobbers strove to create a tulipo-mania. In both cities they only partially succeeded. However, the force of example brought the flowers into great favour, and amongst a certain class of people tulips have ever since been prized more highly than any other flowers of the field. The Dutch are still notorious for their partiality to them, and con-tinue to pay higher prices for them than any other people. As the rich Englishman boasts of his fine race-horses or his old pic-tures, so does the wealthy Dutchman vaunt him of his tulips.

In England, in our day, strange as it may appear, a tulip will produce more money than an oak. If one could be found, *rara in terris,* and black as the black swan of Juvenal, its price would equal that of a dozen acres of standing corn. In Scotland, towards the close of the seventeenth century, the highest price for tulips, according to the authority of a writer in the supple-ment to the third edition of the *Encyclopedia Britannica,* was ten guineas. Their value appears to have diminished from that time till the year 1769, when the two most valuable species in England were the *Don Quevedo* and the *Valentinier,* the former of which was worth two guineas and the latter two guineas and a half. These prices appear to have been the minimum. In the year 1800, a common price was fifteen guineas for a single bulb. In 1835, a bulb of the species called the Miss Fanny Kem-ble was sold by public auction in London for seventy-five pounds. Still more remarkable was the price of a tulip in the possession of a gardener in the King's Road, Chelsea;—in his catalogues it was labelled at two hundred guineas.

Confusión de Confusiones

Joseph de la Vega
1688

INTRODUCTION

WHOEVER comes to know Joseph Penso de la Vega's *Confusión de Confusiones* will recognize at once that he is concerned with a literary oddity. Here is a book written in Spanish by a Portuguese Jew, published in Amsterdam, cast in dialogue form, embellished from start to finish with biblical, historical, and mythological allusions, and yet concerned primarily with the business of the stock exchange and issued as early as 1688. Such a volume obviously requires a good deal of explaining.

I

Let us begin by identifying the ethnic group to which the author belonged. This was the Sephardic community of Amsterdam, the term "Sephards" being given to those Jews whose ancestors had lived on the Iberian peninsula—in contrast to the term "Ashkenasim," which was used to designate Jews of central or eastern European origin. During the fifteenth century great pressure was exerted by the Church authorities in Spain and Portugal to induce the Jews (and equally the Moors) resident there to accept Christianity. Some did, but many merely went through the necessary motions and secretly retained their earlier faith. When in 1492 the unconverted Jews (and Moors) were expelled from Spain, many fled to Portugal; but in 1536 the Portuguese also introduced the Inquisition, and the recent immigrants had to look elsewhere for asylum. Many of the purely nominal Christians, the "Christianos nuevos," as they were called in Spain, joined their more stiff-backed brethren in these pilgrimages. It is probably also true, relative to the second migration, that some of the Jews in Spain and Portugal were attracted to the cities of northern

---

This is the introduction by Hermann Kellenbenz as published in the 1957 reprint of this title.

Europe by the economic opportunities there offered to their entrepreneurial skills.

At all events, the de la Vega family seems to have been numbered among the "new Christians." An earlier generation had moved to Portugal; then, perhaps after 1536, it returned to Spain; and finally, a hundred years later, about 1630, it migrated to the Low Countries. It found substantial colonies already settled on the banks of the lower Elbe and the lower Amstel, where the members could, of course, live openly according to their traditions. The first immigrants of this character had appeared at the close of the fifteenth century; the stream had increased in size in the succeeding century; and by the time of the appearance of our *Confusión de Confusiones* the Sephardic communities of northern Europe had in fact reached what was to constitute the height of their influence in that area. The major part of these colonies spoke the Portuguese language, since that was the official language of their congregations. Therefore their members came to be referred to by the Gentiles as "Portuguese" or "Portuguese Jews." However, curiously enough, those of the group who acquired literary ambitions chose to write their poems, plays, legal treatises, and other works in Spanish. Presumably a larger proportion of the educated element knew Spanish rather than either Portuguese or Dutch, or else Spanish was a language common to all these elements, whatever their native language.

In Amsterdam the Sephardic immigrants had greater economic opportunities and greater liberties than in Hamburg, and soon the Amsterdam Sephardic settlement outshone that of the town on the Elbe. However, any statement regarding the greater liberties granted to the Sephardic Jews in Amsterdam must be understood within the general context of seventeenth-century life in Europe. Church and guilds there imposed various types of restrictions upon Jewish activities. For example, an Amsterdam decree of March 29th, 1632 forbade the Jews to participate in any occupation practiced by members of the local guilds. Jews could not obtain membership in any of them. They were not allowed to peddle goods or to have retail shops.

Craftsmanship was open to them only in lines that were related to the ritual of their religion, or that had not been organized into guilds. By the terms of these exceptions, they could become butchers, poulterers, and bakers, and they could find occupation in such a handicraft as the cutting of diamonds. Above all, wholesale trade in goods and shipping enterprises stood open to them. A certain number of them were allowed to practice the profession of broker, while others could engage in money lending, money changing, and the like.

Until recently, the economic importance of the Portuguese Jewish settlement in Amsterdam has tended to be exaggerated by scholars, but such ideas have been corrected by new research. The progress in their financial circumstances, the amount of their wealth at various times, and the magnitude of their largest holdings in comparison with those of the largest non-Sephardic enterprises are all well reflected in the accounts of the Bank of Amsterdam and in the registers of the tax returns of 1631, 1674, and 1743. We see from these newly opened sources that *de facto* the largest fortunes and the largest financial transactions were those of the indigenous families of the regents and patricians. However, it is true that the proportion of the "Portuguese" population which participated in the economic life of Amsterdam was greater than that of the other ethnic group. Recent investigations have also shown that the prosperity of this Portuguese people derived primarily from merchandise trading: the importation of sugar, spices, salt, dye woods, jewels, and precious metals from the South, and the exportation of Northern raw materials and particularly of valuable finished goods in return.*

However, there seems to have been a considerable tendency for these "Portuguese" to participate in the financial activities of the city, including outright speculation. Surely the

---

* We shall not have really satisfactory knowledge of the size of Sephardic commerce until the many documents of Amsterdam notaries preserved in the Gemeente-Archief have been made available, a work which is now being carried forward by the archivist Dr. S. Hart and his assistants.

civic regulations under which they lived at least opened the door in that direction, but there is also the fact that Jews who had had, as crypto-Christians, good connections with the markets for goods in the Iberian countries, would quite likely lose such contacts when they had returned to their original faith and had migrated to distant lands. Leastways, a contemporary of Joseph de la Vega—a knowledgeable "Englishman Gentleman" writing in 1701 in his *Description of Holland*—stated that "the Jews are the chief in that Trade [of stock speculation], and are said to Negotiate 17 parts in 20" of the main business, that of trading in shares of the East India Company. Accordingly, there is good reason to believe that Joseph de la Vega as a member of the Amsterdam Jewish community had satisfactory access to information about the speculation in shares in that city.

II

The first documentary trace that we have of the de la Vega family itself relates to its existence in Spain. Isaac Penso or Isaac Penso Felix, our author's father, was born in Spain in 1608, and at the time was living as a "Christiano nuevo" in Espejo, a little place in the province of Cordoba. His family must quite surely have come from Portugal, since the name "Penso" is of Portuguese or Gallego origin. There are several villages with the name Penso in northern Portugal and in Galicia. Moreover, the name of another family from which Isaac Penso could claim descendancy was that of "Passarinho," which is a Portuguese word meaning "little bird." Actually there seem to have been a number of Portuguese "new Christian" families that moved (or moved back) to Spain in the course of the 16th century, especially during those years when Portugal was a part of Spain.

Isaac Penso married Esther de la Vega.* Their first son, Abraham, took his father's surname, but their second son,

---

* They had four sons and six daughters. While two of the sons passed their lives in Amsterdam, the others emigrated to London. All four of them became related by marriage to the family of Alvares Vega in Antwerp. These several family ties were increased when a daughter of Isaac Penso also married into the same Vega family.

Joseph, who became the author of the *Confusion,* took that of his mother, after the tradition of his people. Therefore, our author's full name was Joseph Penso de la Vega Passarinho, with sometimes the addition of the other surname Felix. But he generally used the shortened form of Joseph de la Vega.

The father, Isaac Penso, was so unfortunate as to have gained some experience with the prison of the Inquisition, and he is known to have vowed, if and when released, to return to the faith of his ancestors. When he was in fact freed, he actually emigrated to Antwerp, where he would be permitted to carry out his vow, and which, as late as the seventeenth century, still had a fairly large Portuguese colony, consisting in an important degree of descendants of new Christians. Subsequently, Isaac Penso lived for a time in Hamburg, to which other members of the family had migrated. One Joseph Penso, whose name can be found in the Hamburg records as early as 1647, was perhaps a brother. As to the place of Isaac Penso within the Hamburg Portuguese community, it is noteworthy that he was elected "parnas," i.e., elder, for the year of 1655. Soon he moved to Amsterdam. Here he is supposed to have been occupied principally in the banking business. At all events, he became a well-to-do man and associated with the most respected members of the Jewish community. He was elected to several posts, he opened his house for religious meetings, he distinguished himself by his beneficence, and he participated in the establishment of one of the numerous Talmudic "academies" in which the study of Mosaic law was cultivated.*

III

The date and place of Joseph's birth cannot be established with surety. Apparently he was born about 1650, possibly while his parents were still staying at Espejo, but more probably after they

---

*When he died in 1683, worthies such as Chacham Aboab and Dr. Sarphati de Pina honored him with commemorative discourses, and the poet, Daniel Levi de Barrios, as well as his own son, our Joseph, composed funeral orations upon his character and his accomplishments.

had moved to northern Europe. While a youth, he spent some time in Leghorn, and then established himself at Amsterdam, although also visiting Hamburg rather frequently. Soon he attracted attention by his literary talents. In 1667, when only about 17 years old, he made himself known through the composition of a Hebrew drama entitled *Asire ha Tikwah* or *The Prisoner of Hope,* which was praised as the beginning of a new epoch of Hebrew poetry. It was published in Amsterdam in 1673.

Although in his earlier years directed by his family toward the career of a rabbi, Joseph actually became a businessman. He managed his business activities, however, in such a way that he had considerable time available for writing; and in his leisure he composed marriage poems, poems in praise of princes, novels, speeches, and treatises of moral and philosophical character. He became a member of the Academia de los Sitibundos founded in 1676 by the Spanish Resident Manuel de Belmonte, and he served on its jury, a body which passed judgment on, and awarded prizes to, poems submitted to it. When Belmonte in 1685 founded a literary debating club called the Academia de los Foridos, de la Vega became its secretary. Journeys to Antwerp, where his wife had been born and where several of his works were published, to Leghorn, and possibly to Espejo, widened his intellectual horizon. His contemporaries praised his scholarship, his powers of fantasy, his talent for language and literary form.

Despite considerable scholarly research, no one has been able to establish with assurance a complete list of the works of Joseph de la Vega. In the preface to a collection of his novels entitled *Rumbos Peligrosos,* or *Dangerous Travels,* which were published in 1683, he stated that over the years he had written two hundred letters to princes and friends about subjects interesting to students of historical as well as contemporary affairs; these he had written to the grateful as well as the mournful and the dissatisfied, the lovers and the gay, the preachers, the moralists, and the poets. Among his more notable productions—beyond the drama already mentioned—were an *Oracion Funebre* for his mother and another one for his father, both of which were printed in Amsterdam in 1683. To Manuel

Teixeira, the Hamburg Resident of Queen Christina of Sweden, he dedicated a speech which he delivered the same year in the Academia de los Sitibundos, while he honored the Portuguese agent Mose Curiel, alias Jeronimo Nunes da Costa, with a panegyric on the divine law of Moses. Another panegyric offered on the occasion of the liberation of Vienna from the assault of the Turks was addressed to the King of Poland, Jan Sobieski. In the year 1683, there appeared the collection of novels called *Rumbos Peligrosos* or *Dangerous Travels,* already noted. They were written after Italian models and were supposed to sparkle by reason of their new pretentious style. In 1685, de la Vega published the speeches that he had made in the Academia de los Floridos. Then chronologically came de la Vega's most remarkable product. This was the book of dialogues concerned with the operations of the stock exchange of Amsterdam, and the book which interests us, his *Confusión de Confusiones,* issued in 1688. In 1690 he dedicated a little work to King William III of England; while his last known publication, a speech dedicated to the Portuguese ambassador in the Hague, Diego de Mendoza Corte Real, bore the date of the 15th of March, 1692. Soon afterwards he is supposed to have died. He was buried, like his father, in the cemetery at Oudekerk on the Amstel.

IV

It was on the 24th of May, 1688, when Joseph de la Vega, following a custom of his time, signed a dedication to his dialogues on the business of the stock exchange of Amsterdam. It was directed to Duarte Nunes de Costa, an honored member of the Portuguese community in that city. The latter's grandfather, Duarte, and his father, Jeronimo, had rendered important services in Hamburg and Amsterdam as agents of King John IV in the years of the Portuguese restoration. Jeronimo belonged to the group of the Amsterdam congregation which, in 1673, had laid the corner-stone for the new synagogue there. As already mentioned, de la Vega had dedicated to him a panegyric in 1683. Now, *his* son Duarte (in the community called Jacob) was honored by the dedication of the book on the operation of the exchange in Amsterdam. One has only to look at this dedication to obtain a good idea of the flowery, affected style, of which de la Vega was so proud. It surpassed the usual profuseness of the writers of his time. He there wove a garland of fanciful suggestions and comparisons around the word "acciones" (stocks); he played with the word "costa" (coast), so as to allude to the addressee, and with the word "paxaro" which reminded him of his own line of ancestors. In the same style he proceeded in the prologue and finally in the text of the book. The four dialogues among a philosopher, a merchant, and a shareholder, intended to present a picture of life on the exchange, are interrupted time and again by light and contrived, if scholarly, excursions into the realms of mythology, philosophy, the Old Testament, and classical poetry. In so doing, de la Vega aimed at "a new style that imitated nobody, in order not to be imitated by anybody," but he actually went to extremes. The "estilo culto," which was his goal, turned out to have been complicated and affected, and for that reason alone lacked contemporary imitators, while for people of the present day its products are often very difficult to understand.

The author stressed in the preface to his book that he had three motives in writing the dialogues: first, his own pleasure; again, for those who were not active in the trade, he desired to describe a business which was on the whole the most honest and most useful of all that existed at that time; and, lastly, he wished to describe accurately and fully the tricks that rascals knew how to employ in that business. In this last connection his purpose was in part to warn people against entering into the speculation by acquainting them with the deceitful measures, but especially to unmask the evildoers. He compared the life on the exchange to a labyrinth, and assured the reader that he certainly did not exaggerate: what he wrote might give the impression of a hyperbole or extravagance, but it was really no more than a true description of the conditions. He called the dialogues *Confusion of Confusions* because there was no rational purpose in the activities which was not overlaid with an irrational one, no trick used by one person which others did not pay back with the same coin, so that, in this stock-exchange business, one moved in a world of darkness which nobody wholly understood and no pen was able really to describe in all its intricacies.

In view of these complexities, the literary form which de la Vega chose—the dialogue—was wholly appropriate. The hypothetical discussion permitted the author to expose the various aspects of the problem, and indeed to do so without the dullness of straight exposition. The form also fitted de la Vega's particular relationship to the materials which he sought to present. He could adopt and maintain an apparent objectivity, and yet could give expression to his own opinions by putting them into the mouth of one or more of his characters. It has generally been held that the "shareholder" is usually the vehicle for the pronouncement of the author's judgments. Actually, of course, the dialogue as a literary form had had a long history in 1688, having been utilized in the Bible and in classical writings, of which latter perhaps the most famous examples were Plato's *Dialogues*. More recently, the literary form of dialogue had been revived in the Renaissance by Petrarch, Erasmus, and others. If de la Vega had been looking at Spanish authors, he could have located examples easily, e.g., in the writings of the Marquess of Santillana, of Juan de Valdes, or of Cervantes, whose *Coloquio de los Perros* or *Colloquium of the Dogs* was (and is) a famous piece of literature. Even highly technical questions were at this period presented in the form of dialogues. One may refer to Machiavelli's *Dell' Arte della Guerra (On the Art of War)* of 1519/20.

V

When de la Vega published his book, the trade and speculation in stocks had not existed the length of a single century. To be sure, speculation in goods was older. As early as the middle of the sixteenth century, people in Amsterdam speculated in grain and, somewhat later, in herring, spices, whale-oil, and even tulips. The Amsterdam bourse in particular was the place where this kind of business was carried on. This institution began as an open-air market in Warmoestreet, later moved for a while to the "New Bridge," which crosses the Damrak, then flourished in the "church square" near the Oude Kerk until the Amsterdam merchants built their own exchange building in 1611.

Trade and speculation in shares first appeared there when, in 1602, the six local "chambers" for East Indian trade were united into a general Dutch East India Company. According to the official pronouncement, every inhabitant of the United Provinces had an opportunity to participate in the Company. At the beginning the rights deriving from the initial payments were called "paerten," "partieen," or "partijen," the words being taken over from the practice of "participation" in the shipping business. It was not until 1606 that the word "actie" (i.e., share) seems to have come into use. The possibility of trading in these "participations" was assured by the fact that each owner of shares could, by payment of a fee, transfer his holdings, in whole or in part, to another person. The chapter of Amsterdam subscribed more than half of the total sum contributed by the several chapters; and, with that proportion of "ownership" continuing subsequently, it was in Amsterdam that the trading in shares flourished most luxuriantly.

Only a few days after the original subscription had been completed, the shares of the Dutch East India Company were being traded in so actively that they rose to 14 or 15 per cent above par; and the tendency to rise continued until by 1607 the price had almost doubled. However, in the following year the market value fell to 130 per cent of par, as a consequence of manipulations by a group of speculators organized by one Isaac Le Maire, who ultimately were concerned with the founding of a rival French company. These early stock-market "operators" sold large blocks of shares and, in addition, sought to depress the price both by selling "short" and by spreading rumors that were unfavorable to the Dutch Company. Consequently, on the 27th of February 1610, the first edict was published prohibiting activities of this sort, especially the "windhandel," that is, the dealing in shares that were not in the possession of the seller. The sale of shares of the Company by *bona fide* owners for future delivery was allowed. In 1621, after the outbreak of war with Spain, a second edict against the "wind trade" had to be issued, and further prohibitions followed; but apparently the abuses could not be eliminated.

The volume of trading seems to have varied as greatly as the prices and the resort to "rigging" of the market. As just suggested, the first years after the launching of the East India Company witnessed much speculation. Then there was another period of brisk activity when in 1621 the Dutch West India Company was established, and when its stock also began to be traded in, while thereafter the vicissitudes of the war with Spain and the Thirty Years War kept business rather active over the 1621-1648 period. Then followed a couple of decades of relative quiet, terminated by the speculation that preceded the crisis of 1672. After a lapse of about forty years, a new decree, published in 1677, sought to protect the shareholders of the East India Company.

In the course of the 1680's, trading in stocks seems again to have increased considerably; and for the first time a rather lively public discussion of the problems ensued. In 1687 an Amsterdam lawyer, Nicolaas Muys van Holy, felt himself impelled to publish a pamphlet on the evils of the wind-business. He pointed out that there were professional dealers in stocks who were anxious to worm out the secrets of the State and of the Companies, in order to get the better of ordinary investors through the use of such "inside" information; and, in an effort to reduce speculation, he proposed not only that all sales of stocks be registered but that such sales be taxed. The author was of the opinion that the "Portuguese Nation" was playing a major part in the stock speculation, especially in the speculation in imaginary or fictitious units called "ducaton" shares— of which more shortly. However, his contentions met with strenuous opposition, and several pamphlets were published in criticism of his views. Finally, the magistrate of Amsterdam issued a decree on the 13th of January, 1689, which indeed did levy a tax upon transactions.

It was in this situation of the 1680's that de la Vega's book appeared. Internal evidence shows that the author had personal experience in the business of stock trading. At one place, he says, quite surely in a way of exaggeration, that through speculation in shares he had made fortunes no less than five times and had lost them another five times! If one is able to look through or around the literary peculiarities of the volume, he will find in it a reasonably realistic description of the whole stock market.

De la Vega makes the reader acquainted not only with the history of speculation on the exchange, but also with the various types of speculative transactions used at that time. And, surprisingly enough, we see most of the usages of the stock exchange of today already employed in the 17th century, although not, of course, always known by the same terms. Still, we find expressions such as difference, prolongation, liquidation, limits, brokerage, already in use, expressions which the Dutch with their trade and their financial dealings spread over the world. Also there were speculators for the rise and others speculating for the decline, each with their followers among the brokers.

One expression frequently employed in the *Confusión de Confusiones,* the "appeal to Frederick," has not survived; it had only local and temporary significance. It refers to an often repeated provision in the decrees above-mentioned beginning with that of 1621—really before the time of the Stadholder Frederick Henry. (The provision *was* included in the edicts of 1630 and 1636, edicts of similar character, which were issued while Frederick Henry *was* in office.) By its terms, a buyer of a "short" contract (and perhaps some others) could refuse to adhere to the provisions of it; that is to say, he could repudiate the agreement, and his action would be upheld in the courts of law. Although there seems to have been dispute in the courts as to the variety of individuals and of business transactions that could properly be included within its protection, the intent was quite clearly to increase the hazards of speculation. In a sense, the provision of an "appeal to Frederick" might be regarded as a means of implementing and enforcing the direct prohibition upon "short" sales carried in the edict of 1610, and actually repeated in the subsequent decrees.

De le Vega gives a rather "fuzzy" treatment of these edicts, perhaps because he was not a lawyer; and this points to one of the limitations upon his book: the best that the modern reader can secure from *Confusión de Confusiones* is a "reasonably" realistic picture of the goings-on at the Amsterdam stock exchange. Sometimes de la Vega is inconsistent in his statements, whether because of carelessness (which the author of novels might well manifest) or because of "confusion" in his own mind. Sometimes he appears to exaggerate, possibly for effect, as the author of a drama might. And the course of composition of the book surely goes far to explain—perhaps to excuse—both of these characteristics. Internal evidence tends clearly to show that de la Vega prepared first a sort of manual, possibly for the use of his brothers and others of the "Portuguese nation" who had gone to London, and who quite likely wished to engage in the speculation in stocks that was then just rearing its head in that city, and that subsequently he decided to make a "literary" product out of the original screed. It is striking how, after expurgation of the cerise, if not purple passages, the remaining paragraphs dovetail one another. Possibly the version here offered approximates the original manual, although that end was not part of the initial plan. Finally the book contains some contradictions that derived from the specific circumstance that, between the time when de la Vega began and the time that he completed the writing of the book (or making the revision), a crisis had descended upon the East India Company. A lengthy passage occurs in the fourth dialogue, which narrates this unhappy episode.

On all these counts, incidentally, as also on account of the rather extreme complexities of the transactions described by de la Vega, and sometimes the floweriness of his language, some liberties have been taken in the translation. Words, phrases, occasionally whole sentences have been inserted (in brackets) in the hope of clarifying particular sequences. At other times a rather free rendering has been given of sentences or sections. The scholar will not find a literal translation of the original Spanish, nor of the later German or Dutch versions. However, every effort has, of course, been made to present a true rendering of de la Vega's thoughts.

VI*

An understanding of the data in *Confusión de Confusiones* relative to the operations of the stock exchange at Amsterdam is dependent upon the following explanations of statements or implications to be found on its pages:

1. The security chiefly involved was the stock of the Dutch East India Company—an enterprise that had been launched in 1602 and that had prospered handsomely. The stock of the Dutch West India Company played a much less considerable role. The company was somewhat younger than its East Indian counterpart, having been founded in 1621, and had been less successful. Also it had been reorganized in 1674, and its new shares were perhaps less easily susceptible of manipulation. Obligations of the state are mentioned only once or twice, but seemingly were regularly bought and sold. The East India Company had bonds outstanding but these are not specifically mentioned by de la Vega.

Actually the shares of the West India Company appear to have been bought and sold on a "when issued" basis. An edict of 1621, issued by the States General, asserts, "We understand on good grounds that some men have even sold shares in the forthcoming chartered general company of the West Indies, which shares have yet to be paid up, registered, and transferred, in order to be able to deliver these shares promptly after the creation of the company. This sort of action serves to nullify our authority, resolution, and good intent." This occurred

---

*Because of the technical character of the ensuing section and of the desirability of rendering the material into the American idiom, I have been glad to rely largely upon phraseology supplied by colleagues in this venture, Dr. Cole and Dr. Redlich.

only nineteen years after the formation of the first company with transferrable shares.*

2. The stock of the East India Company had a nominal value of 500 pounds Flemish or 3,000 guilders. It was quoted in 1688 at approximately 580 per cent. Accordingly, the market value of a share of stock at that time was really more than 17,000 guilders. Perhaps this high unit value had something to do with the development of devices for speculation alternative to the *bona fide* purchase and sale of stock.

3. When the company was launched, the stock was taken up by the merchants of several cities in the country. The merchant stock-owners in the several communities were organized into distinct local "chambers," which in turn participated in the governing of the company. Amsterdam possessed the largest portion of the total number of shares, but some of the stock held elsewhere changed hands from time to time, at surprisingly large divergencies from the Amsterdam prices. But de la Vega confines his discussion almost wholly to the Amsterdam situation.

4. The elements in the market at Amsterdam were as follows: wealthy investors; occasional speculators, mostly merchants of the city; persistent speculators, either in real stock or in a lower-denomination substitute; the Bank of Amsterdam; persons who loaned money with stock as security (who may also individually have been "wealthy investors"); brokers of various types; "rescounters," for the settlement of "differences" relative to transactions in real shares, and at least one comparable individual who had, until shortly before 1688, adjusted "differences" relative to transactions in the substitute (ducaton) stock.

5. There were various types of transactions in the Amsterdam market.

---

* Also it is revealing of the rapid-fire ingenuity of the Dutch that in this edict there is evidence likewise that buyers and sellers of shares in the East India Company had gotten together to "contract out" of the penalties carried in the preceding edict: they agreed to renounce opportunities to inform the authorities and get a portion of the fine.

a. There were sales of the real stock against immediate payment of cash.

b. There were comparable sales where the money to cover payments was borrowed from individuals, up to four-fifths of its value.

c. There were transactions in which future settlement dates were specified—that is, beyond the regular monthly settlement dates. These future contracts were seemingly used for both speculative and hedging purposes, both by the speculators and by the lenders on securities. De la Vega implies that the latter parties always hedged by means of such contracts. Hypothecation, which was mentioned as early as 1610 (in the edict of that year), was permitted to the seller presumably during the period of the forward contract.* Arrangements also were possible, and were fairly frequently resorted to, whereby the date of the termination of a future contract could be postponed, apparently by mutual consent of the parties. This action was called "prolongation."

A large proportion of the foregoing future sales were really sales "in blanco"—or short sales, as we would label them—even though such transactions were prohibited by laws of the state and of the city.

d. There were option contracts. These were at least of the "call" and "put" varieties, which have persisted ever since, where a party agrees to deliver a given amount of stock at a specified price upon "call" by the co-contracting party at a specified time, and where a party agrees to accept a given amount of stock at a specific time and price if it is "put" upon him then. (These are obviously also future contracts of a sort.) De la Vega implies at one or two points that there were likewise contracts of the "straddle" type, i.e., where one party to the contract agrees *either* to deliver or accept stock at a specified time and price; but the author is not clear on the point.

In all cases of "call" or "put" agreements, a premium was paid by the buyer of the privilege. The amount of the premium

---

* [The purchaser could also hypothecate; see below, pp. 5 and 24—ed.]

was dependent upon a number of circumstances: the length (in time) of the contract; the judgment of the seller of the contract as to the likelihood of the movement of the stock values in question; seemingly the number of such contracts being negotiated at the time; and other, not-unimportant factors.

Option contracts were utilized sometimes for hedging purposes by *bona fide* investors, but more commonly for mere speculation. The purchaser of a "call" contract (as in the case of present-day "futures" on our commodity exchanges) was not usually interested really in acquiring the stock at the specified time and price, but in the difference between the price in the contract and that which might come to prevail in the market by the date specified in the contract. The same could be said of the person who used an option contract for hedging purposes: he was not interested in receiving or giving shares.

e. In addition there were purchases and sales of "ducaton" shares. (Such transactions were of recent origin in 1688, and actually had been abandoned in the slump that had occurred just as de la Vega was writing his book.) What this "ducaton" trading amounted to is a bit uncertain on the strength of what de la Vega actually says. Scholars who have worked on this period assert that the ducaton shares were fictitious. Yet de la Vega surely speaks of traders who had "bought large shares and sold ducaton shares" as well as of others who had "bought ducaton shares" because they had "sold large shares." Here, to be sure, de la Vega may be using the words "bought" and "sold" as a sort of shorthand for taking a long or a short position.

At all events the best authorities assure us that in such dealings the "stock" had a nominal value of a tenth that of the real East India shares. No delivery of securities was expected, of course, and the point of the whole business was the calculation of profit or loss at a monthly settlement date. Documents covering these transactions were actually executed between the parties. At the settlement day specified in the agreement, the "difference" between the anticipated and the actual values was paid by the party who had guessed wrong. The whole business was a form of gambling on the future course of the stock market, the course of ducaton values being more or less closely linked with that of real shares.

De la Vega describes how, for settlement purposes, the value of the fictitious stock was determined on the day appointed, namely, by the declaration of two respected individuals. At one point the author mentions the excitement and confusion on the exchange when this price was due to be ascertained and disclosed. Apparently an official of the exchange put a legal termination to the transactions to be included within the given period by raising a stick as a signal. Some folk wanted the raising of the stick delayed, others to have it speeded up; and seemingly the speculators gave loud vent to their respective desires.

De la Vega also asserts at one point that street-corner speculators who could not afford to buy and sell ducaton shares, did so in shares with a still lower value; but he may here have been indulging in hyperbole.

6. It is worth special note that much of the speculation was of a different character from that to which most Americans are accustomed. At least the mental construction is different. In America, because of daily settlements, one thinks in terms of actual purchases and sales, even if some of the transactions can take place only by the use of borrowed stock. In seventeenth-century Amsterdam—and indeed in all of Europe over later centuries—the speculators thought in terms of the "difference" between what one anticipated and what actually occurred: the "difference" between what one agreed to pay, to sell at, to deliver stock at, or receive it at, and what one found at the stipulated time to have become the prevailing value.

The system of monthly settlements provided a fertile ground for the development of this mode of thought, and of action. One could make several moves, could shift positions, &c., and some of his transactions would balance or "wash out" others.

The possibility of this sort of "clearing" was the origin of the "rescounters" mentioned by de la Vega. He describes these men as brokers who "make it their business to balance out or 'rescounter' the commitments [of the speculators, it seems] and to pay and to receive the differences." Although the "rescontran-ten" have been reported as dating from early in the seventeenth century, de la Vega's description carries the implication that the activity was of recent development. Surely the latter does not explain how such clearing agents could function in so large a market as he sometimes suggests to have obtained.

The same sort of operation was carried out by the "general cashier," mentioned by de la Vega, in supervising and recording the contracts relative to ducaton shares.

7. As already suggested, settlement of indebtednesses came once a month. For real stock, the closing date was the 20th, with actual payment due on the 25th. For ducaton shares, settlements seem to have come at the first of each month, although de la Vega at one place indicates that they came both at the beginning and at the middle of each month.

8. Balances at the Bank of Amsterdam were apparently utilized much in effecting payments. Stocks are spoken of as "payable at the Bank," and the premiums on option contracts are alleged to have been "transferred immediately at the Bank."

The Bank also maintained what de la Vega speaks of as "time accounts" for its customers. These seem to have been in the nature of quasi-official records kept in connection with the monthly settlement procedure, time agreements, and the government's efforts to eliminate short sales (of which more will be said in a moment). Seemingly a seller could demonstrate that he was not selling short by giving a proper notification to the Bank, which would retain it until payment had been actually made. Similar "time accounts" appear to have also been maintained at the Bank when the purchaser of stock was borrowing part of the purchase price.

The stock of the Company did not pass from hand to hand; it was not negotiable paper. A sale of stock or other transfer could be effected only by the appearance of the two parties, buyer and seller, at the offices of the Company, and by the entering of the proper data on the Company's books by the enterprise's secretary. (This was once also the procedure necessary in the transfer of balances held with private bankers or early commercial banks, a procedure which has left its trace in the Continental *giro* procedures, and in the wording of modern checks, "Pay to the order of" so-and-so.)

9. Purchases and sales were often (but not necessarily) effected through brokers, who were of several sorts. One division was that of sworn and free brokers. The former were licensed by the government, were limited in number, and were forbidden to trade on their own accounts. The latter were more numerous and, although not checked so closely by the government as the sworn brokers, are actually given a good rating by de la Vega.

Another division was that between brokers for the bulls and those for the bears. Whether both sworn and free brokers formed such alliances is not stated, nor is it clear why the allegiances came into existence. The circumstance, frequently illustrated, of intense rivalry between the bull and bear factions may have had some bearing, as is intimated by de la Vega, but also there could have been reason in the trading carried on by the free brokers on their own account. Perhaps the speculators sometimes found the brokers to be real allies. However, the author gives cases of brokers switching sides as if allegiances were not rigidly held.

10. Transactions were completed at various places in Amsterdam. Trading was general at a specific outdoor area near the old Dam in the forenoons, and in the Exchange building in the early afternoons. However, the author gives cases of deals negotiated elsewhere: at coffee houses, in private houses, even perhaps in bed!

11. Indeed the effective legal restraints on the dealings in securities seem to have been few.

a. A man who failed to meet his legitimate obligations could be declared a bankrupt; but that would be true of dealings in commodities, land, etc.

b. Efforts were made to prevent the stock-brokers, free as well as sworn, from dealing on their own account; the law was enforced enough, it seems, so that the sworn brokers abided by it, while the free brokers sometimes established nominally separate enterprises through which to do their speculating. On the other hand, de la Vega implies throughout that many brokers actually did speculate for their own advantage.

c. As already suggested, a real endeavor seems to have been made to eliminate short selling. The States General had issued an edict forbidding all such agreements, in the first days of stock trading in the Netherlands, as early as 1610; and this edict had been reissued from time to time. And there had been edicts issued since the 1620's allowing speculators to "appeal to Frederick," i.e., repudiate contracts of certain types.

However, enforcement was left to the market itself. No officers seem to have felt it their duty to intervene; and de la Vega gives no instance of official action by anybody, except the determination of cases in the courts—cases which were probably initiated by individuals. What happened was that any speculator who found himself over-extended in transactions which were technically illegal, could "appeal to Frederick"; and apparently some speculators did so.

But the types of transaction supposedly covered by the edicts were still uncertain in 1688; the decisions of the courts were not clear. De la Vega spends an appreciable time endeavoring to show what lines had been drawn. Clearly dealings in ducaton or other fictitious units were outlawed; option contracts were surely suspect; and even sellers of real stock would be wise to demonstrate the legality of their operations in the case of time sales, as by use of the purchasers' "time accounts" at the company offices. This sort of escrow arrangement, set up as early as 1613, was intended to protect against the "appeal" possessors of stock who chose to sell on time.

The general objective of the edicts seems to have been to prevent or eliminate artificial depressing of the market value of shares—"rigging the market" in more modern phrase—and the authorities went about it by forbidding sales by anyone of something that he did not actually possess and agreeing to stand behind repudiations of the forbidden variety of contract. A prohibition of the same sort as that of 1610 and later years had actually been used first in the commodity markets, and only subsequently extended to cover stock transactions.

VII

Finally the questions of value or significance may be raised; what effect at the time did the *Confusión* have? And what purposes subsequently has this book served? Of the first matter, very little is known. The facts that the book was written in Spanish rather than in the language—Dutch—which most of the speculators or others concerned with the stock market must have used, and that its form was altered from that of a straightforward manual into an extravagant literary piece— both these facts would surely have militated against its having wide reading or wide impact upon the ideas or legislative purposes of de la Vega's contemporaries. Possibly also the crisis that hit the market while the author was still busy with his pen, and the tax upon sales imposed the succeeding year, combined to dampen the spirit of speculation for a while, until *Confusión de Confusiones* had been forgotten. No part of it seems to have been translated into Dutch until the whole book was so treated by historical scholars of the 20th century.

For students of economic and business history, however, including those responsible for the Dutch translation of 1939, the volume has been of signal value. No other book deals as extensively as *Confusión de Confusiones* with the trading in stocks at Amsterdam, and nowhere else in the world of the seventeenth century was there so mature a business of this sort as existed then at Amsterdam. And surely the significance of the volume is not lessened by the circumstance that through a perusal of de la Vega's book one learns how rapidly the trading in stocks became sophisticated; indeed, how in a few decades the Dutch, aided perhaps by members of the "Portuguese nation," found it possible to devise both procedures and stratagems which modern operators have scarcely been able to better.

HERMANN KELLENBENZ

Würzburg, January, 1957.

CONFUSIÓN DE CONFUSIONES

First Dialogue

[At the beginning of the book, the merchant speaks of the emblems of Mercury, the god of the merchants, as constituting good symbols for the activities of his fellow businessmen. The philosopher, with witty metaphors based on the words "cash," "bank," and other business terms, stresses, in contrast, the tranquillity of a savant's life. The shareholder breaks in, leading the discussion to a specific form of business, that in stocks, whereupon the philosopher raises a question:]

Philosopher: And what kind of business is this about which I have often heard people talk but which I neither understand nor have ever made efforts to comprehend? And I have found no book that deals with the subject and makes apprehension easier.

Shareholder: I really must say that you are an ignorant person, friend Greybeard, if you know nothing of this enigmatic business which is at once the fairest and most deceitful in Europe, the noblest and the most infamous in the world, the finest and the most vulgar on earth. It is a quintessence of academic learning and a paragon of fraudulence; it is a touchstone for the intelligent and a tombstone for the audacious, a treasury of usefulness and a source of disaster, and finally a counterpart of Sisyphus who never rests as also of Ixion who is chained to a wheel that turns perpetually.

Philosopher: Does my curiosity not deserve a short description from you of this deceit and a succinct explication of this riddle?

Merchant: That is my wish also, because the importunities of instructions, the shipment of goods, and the circulation of bills of exchange are all so burdensome to me. This load of work leads me to look for another means of acquiring a fortune and, even at the risk of loss, to slough off these many wearisome activities.

Shareholder: The best and most agreeable aspect of the new business is that one can become rich without risk. Indeed, without endangering your capital, and without having anything to do with correspondence, advances of money, warehouses, postage, cashiers, suspensions of payment, and other unforeseen incidents, you have the prospect of gaining wealth if, in the case of bad luck in your transactions, you will only change your name. Just as the Hebrews, when they are seriously ill, change their names in order to obtain relief, so a changing of his name is sufficient for the speculator who finds himself in difficulties, to free himself from all impending dangers and tormenting disquietude.

Philosopher: And which name does he assume? The name of Philip, Leonardo, or Diego?

Shareholder: No, there is no need, in order to save himself, for him to take to his heels or, as the saying is, "to adopt the stockings of Villa Diego."* It is enough to refer to the name of Frederick† in order to escape terror and to suppress all pursuit. . . .

I will fulfill your wish to be informed about the origin of this business, and you will see that the stocks do not exist merely for fools but also for intelligent people.

In 1602 a few Dutch merchants founded a company. The wealthiest people [in the country] took an interest in it, and a total capital of sixty-four and a third tons of gold [or more than 6.4 million florins] was raised. Several ships were built and in

---

*The Spanish proverb here cited has two forms, *Tomarlas de Villadiego* or *Tomar las Calzas de Villadiego,* meaning to flee headlong. Villa Diego is a place in the province of Burgos. The Jews living there used *calzas* a kind of knee-breeches; and, so clad, they could flee readily from their Castillian persecutors.

† The name here should really be Frederick Henry. See Introduction.

1604 were sent out to seek adventure Quixote-like in the East Indies. The property of the Company was broken into several parts, and each part (called an *actie* [share], carrying the possibility of acting upon [or laying a claim to] the surplus or profits) amounted to 500 pounds [Flemish] or 3,000 florins.* There were many, however, who did not subscribe to a whole share, but took only a smaller portion according to their wealth, inclination, or expectation of the future. The ships sailed their courses without encountering windmills or enchanted giants. Their successful voyages, their victorious conquests, and the rich return cargoes meant that Caesar's *Veni, vidi, vici* was surpassed and that a tidy profit was made—which became a stimulus to further undertakings. The first distribution of the profit was postponed till 1612 in order to increase the company's capital. Then the administration distributed 57½ per cent, while in 1613 the dividends amounted to 42½ per cent—so that the shareholders, after having had their capital paid back to them, could enjoy any further return as so much velvet.

Gradually the company developed to such an extent that it surpassed the most brilliant enterprises which have ever been famous in the history of the world. Every year new shipments and new riches arrive, [the proceeds from] which are distributed as profits or are utilized in expenditures in accordance with the stipulations of the administration. (The dividends are sometimes paid in cloves, sometimes in [promissory] notes, at other times in money, just as the directors think fit.) From the founding of the Company to the date of this conversation, the dividends have amounted to 1,482½ per cent, while the value of the capital has increased more than five-fold. This treasure is compared to a tree, because it yields fruits [almost] every year, and, although during some years it has only produced blossoms, there have been other years when it has resembled the trees of Uraba† which display their fruitfulness two or three times a

---

*Hereafter the author's references to "pounds" will be understood to mean Flemish pounds.

† Uraba is a province in Columbia.

year, and which competed with the Sibylines* whose branches were of gold and whose leaves were of emeralds. Others call the Company the tree of the knowledge of good and evil, such as exists in Paradise, because it is kept informed of everything that happens along all the branches [of its interests]. However, I have come to see that it resembles the tree of life, because innumerable men earn their living in its shadow. And those who are satisfied with the fruits, and do not insist on pulling up the roots . . . , will admit that they do pretty well in such a business.

Philosopher: I think I have fully grasped *usque ad ultimas differentias* the meaning of the Company, its shares, its principles, its reputation, its splendor, its initiation, its progress, its administration, the distribution of profits, and its stability. But what has this to do with that mysterious business you mentioned, with the tricks you pointed out, with the difficulties you emphasized, with the entire exclusion of risk, with the changing of names, and with other exaggerations and expressions which have filled me with perplexity, rapture, and confusion? . . .

Shareholder: [Let me return to my assertions] that this business of mine is a mysterious affair, and that, even as it was the most fair and noble in all of Europe, so it was also the falsest and most infamous business in the world. The truth of this paradox becomes comprehensible, when one appreciates that this business has necessarily been converted into a game, and merchants [concerned in it] have become speculators. Had the conversion of these merchants into speculators been the only change, the harm would have been bearable, but, what is worse, a portion of the stock brokers have become card-sharpers and, though they are familiar with the blossoms, they nevertheless lose the fruits.[†]

---

* The comment on the Sibylines may well have been taken from one of the fabulous books of travels, a type of literature of which many specimens were published in the epoch of the discoveries.

[†] Here the author is indulging in a play on words, since in Spanish *flor* means both "flower," and a "trick" of a card-sharp.

For a better understanding of this notable fact, it should be observed that three classes of men are to be distinguished on the stock exchange. The princes of business belong to the first class, the merchants to the second, and the speculators to the last.

Every year the financial lords and the big capitalists enjoy the dividends from the shares that they have inherited or have bought with money of their own. They do not care about movements in the price of the stock. Since their interest lies not in the sale of the stock but in the revenues secured through the dividends, the higher value of the shares forms only an imaginary enjoyment for them, arising from the reflection . . . that they could in truth obtain a high price if they were to sell their shares.

The second class is formed by merchants who buy a share (of 500 pounds) and have it transferred on their name (because they are expecting favorable news from India or of a peace treaty in Europe). They sell these shares when their anticipations come true and when the price rises. Or they buy shares against cash, but try to sell them immediately for delivery at a later date, when the price will be higher (i.e., for which date a higher price is already quoted). They do this from fear of changes in the [political or economic] situation or of the arrival of [unfavorable] information, and are satisfied with [what amounts to] the interest on their [temporarily] invested money. They consider their risk as much as their profit; they prefer to gain little, but to gain that little with [relative] security; to incur no risk other than the solvency of the other party in this forward contract; and to have no worries other than those bound up with unforeseen events.

Gamblers and speculators belong to the third class. They have tried to decide all by themselves about the magnitude of their gains and, in order to do so, . . . they have put up wheels of fortune. Oh, what double-dealers! Oh, what an order of life has been created by these schemers! The labyrinth of Crete was no more complicated than the labyrinth of their plans. . . .

They buy one or twenty shares (the latter commitment is usually called a "regiment"), and when the twentieth of the month approaches (the date of delivery), there are only three possible means of settlement. First there is the sale of the shares, through which profit or loss will arise according to the purchase-price; then there is the hypothecation of the shares to four-fifths of their value (which is done even by the wealthiest traders without harm to their credit); and, finally, the buyer may have the shares transferred to his name and make the purchase price payable at the Bank—which can be done only by very wealthy people, because a "regiment" today costs more than a hundred thousand ducats.

When the date of settlement draws near, and if the shares can neither be taken up by the purchaser nor be hypothecated, they must be sold. The speculators for a decline in prices [i.e., the bears] are aware of this impasse and [try to] bring about a sudden fall in price in order to cause the shares to be sold below purchase-price. [Thus serious difficulties may arise for some of the speculators] . . .

Several among those who are in difficulties (immoral people, of course) know how to free themselves through the following argument: *The buyer is not obligated to pay for that which is bought; I lose in the purchase; therefore I am not obliged to pay.*

Philosopher: Ghastly tupidity, unheard-of madness, frightful folly! . . . You assert that the speculator is not obliged to pay for his purchases, but I do not understand the reason for the lack of obligation. I doubt whether he can appeal to a juridical authority such as Bartolus or Baldus.*

Shareholder: This is the chief point and substance of the whole business. Of such complications would not even your Thales know anything, and from your Socrates one could only learn the wisdom that we do not know anything. Therefore I inform you that Solon is not alone as the giver of good laws. Frederick Henry, too, a shining star in the house of Orange-Nassau, promulgated (with wise motives) an ordinance for these provinces, according to which he who sold shares for future

---

*Bartolus (d. 1329) and his disciple Baldus (d. 1400) were important jurists of the 14th century, still highly regarded in the 17th.

delivery without putting them on the time account should be exposed to the danger (because he has sold something he does not own) that the buyer will not take the pieces at the time fixed upon.* When the speculators looked for protection through this recourse (which is called "to appeal to Frederick," in accordance with the name of that famous governor), the storms stopped, the attacks ceased, and the disturbance died down. . . .

Such operations take place in the deep and dangerous waters of the stock exchange, where the swimmers calculate that if the water is reaching up to their necks, they can at best only save their lives. They therefore catch at the first best straw without embarrassment and declare that the art of swimming consists in avoiding dangers. . . . [And the most amusing] thing is that, sometimes before six months have passed, those persons whose money was taken away from them make deals again with those involved in their former business transactions. The fact that money was taken from them serves to establish a credit with which to finance new business transactions, and as a means of their losing more money. When a loss occurs, the losers are expected to pay at least what they have available at the moment, and it might be expected that, as the wound is fresh, there would be no new injury. But though the proverb "He who once is intoxicated . . ."† condemns such goings-on, emotion has greater power than the warning of proverbs; gullibility and seduction cannot in any way be prevented.

I do not say that this frivolity is general, [that is, this "appeal to Frederick," and then more speculation]. There are many persons who refer to the decree [which proclaims the unenforceability of short sales] only when compelled to do so, I mean only if unforeseen losses occur to them in their operations. Other people gradually fulfill their obligations after having sold their last valuables and thus meet with punctuality the reverses of misfortune. But I also knew a friend, a strange man,

---

* See Introduction, p. viii.

† The author is here quoting part of the Spanish proverb, *Quien hace un cesto, hara ciento,* which has the meaning: he who does something once may well get into the habit of doing it.

who recovered from the grief of his loss by pacing up and down in his house, not in order to wake up the dead like Elias, but to bury the living. And after half an hour of such soliloquies he uttered five or six sighs in a tone which betrayed more his relief than his despair. When asked the reason of his joy, which pointed to some sort of compromise that he had come to with his creditors, he answered, "On the contrary, just this moment I have made up my mind not to pay at all, since my peace of mind and my advantage mean more to me than my credit and my honor." I assure you that at this story and at the preposterous and unexpected suggestion I burst out into such a guffaw that I almost shed tears over it. But the fact is that there are many who, . . . like Jonas, snore in the middle of danger; and that, while Adam was ashamed of his nakedness, there are men at the exchange who are not ashamed that (to the disadvantage of their creditors) they have kept hold of their money. . . .

Philosopher: I cannot deny that, in spite of my natural inclination, I would try my fortune [on the exchange] if three great obstacles did not prevent me.

First obstacle: I question whether I should go on board such an endangered ship, to which every wind means a storm and every wave a shipwreck.

Second obstacle: With my limited capital, I could win . . . only if I [were willing to] renounce my reputation frivolously. But to feel degraded . . . without being compensated by wealth, such a thought is vain and insane.

Third obstacle: Preoccupation with this business seems to me unworthy of a philosopher, and, furthermore, since everyone knows the humble character of my surroundings, there would be nobody to give me credit and to have confidence in my beard (for they would see that I cannot pay for stocks on my own account). There would be nobody to lend me money on my beard, as to Don Juan de Castro,* unless it were a beard of gold like that of Aesculapius in the story of Dionysius. . . .

---

*De la Vega here refers to the Portuguese savant and explorer, Juan de Castro, who lived from 1500 to 1548.

Shareholder: Even without going into technicalities I can overcome your doubts. . . . The first danger is removed, because [I can tell you that] there are ropes which secure the vessel against shipwreck and anchors which resist the storm. Give "opsies" or premiums, and there will be only limited risk to you, while the gain may surpass all your imaginings and hopes.

In the light of these precautionary measures, the second objection becomes void. Even if you do not gain through the "opsies" the first time, you do not risk your credit, and do not put your reputation in danger. Therefore, continue to give the premiums for a later date, and it will rarely happen that you lose all your money before a propitious incident occurs that maintains the price for several years. As the contracts are signed because of the premiums and as the payer of the premiums gains in reputation for his generosity as well as for his foresight, keep postponing the terminal dates of your contracts, and keep entering into new ones, so that one contract in time becomes ten, and the business reaches a fine and simple conclusion. If you are [consistently] unfortunate in all your operations and people begin to think that you are shaky, try to compensate for this defect by [outright] gambling in this premium business, [i.e., by borrowing the amount of the premiums]. Since this procedure has become a general practice, you will be able to find someone who will give you credit (and support you in difficult situations, so that you may win without dishonor.)

The third drawback, namely, that it is not proper for a philosopher to speculate, must not concern you, for the exchange resembles the Egyptian temples where every species of animal was worshipped. In the temple of Hercules there were no flies, it is true, but at the stock exchange innumerable men try with Herculean strength to catch the Fly of Money,* and for this purpose many speculators spread poison and invisible threads. . . .

---

*Here again de la Vega introduces a play on words, since the Spanish *mosca* means both "fly" and "money."

If I may explain "opsies" [further, I would say that] through the payment of the premiums, one hands over values in order to safeguard one's stocks or to obtain a profit. One uses them as sails for a happy voyage during a beneficent conjuncture and as an anchor of security in a storm.

The price of the shares is now 580, [and let us assume that] it seems to me that they will climb to a much higher price because of the extensive cargoes that are expected from India, because of the good business of the Company, of the reputation of its goods, of the prospective dividends, and of the peace in Europe. Nevertheless I decide not to buy shares through fear that I might encounter a loss and might meet with embarrassment if my calculations should prove erroneous. I therefore turn to those persons who are willing to take options and ask them how much [premium] they demand for the obligation to deliver shares at 600 each at a certain later date. I come to an agreement about the premium, have it transferred [to the taker of the options] immediately at the Bank, and then I am sure that it is impossible to lose more than the price of the premium. And I shall gain the entire amount by which the price [of the stock] shall surpass the figure of 600.

In case of a decline, however, I need not be afraid and disturbed about my honor nor suffer fright which could upset my equanimity. If the price of the shares hangs around 600, I [may well] change my mind and realize that the prospects are not as favorable as I had presumed. [Now I can do one of two things.] Without danger I [can] sell shares [against time], and then every amount by which they fall means a profit. [Or I can enter into another option contract. In the earlier case] the receiver of the premium was obliged to deliver the stock at an agreed price, and with a rise in the price I could lose only the bonus, so now I can do the same business (in reverse), if I reckon upon a decline in the price of the stock. I now pay premiums for the right to deliver stock at a given price . . . ; or I may cover myself during this period, and often I make a number of successful turns instead of waiting for my luck to come up. But the receiver of the premiums acquires that payment wholly at the determined future date, even if he also runs a risk and pockets the money with fear in his heart.

The Dutch call the option business "opsies," a term derived from the Latin word *optio,* which means choice, because the payer of the premium has the choice of delivering the shares to the acceptor of the premium or of demanding them from him, [respectively].* Since the famous Calepino† derives *optio* or choice, from *optare,* which means to wish, the correct etymology is shown here, because the payer of the premium wishes to choose that which appeals most to him and, in case of misjudgment, he can always avoid that which he had [at first] wanted to choose. . . .

Second Dialogue

Shareholder: In order that you should not come to the conclusion that the movements of the stock exchange are inexplicable and that nothing is firm, take note and realize that there are three causes of a rise in the prices on the exchange and three of a fall: *the conditions in India, European politics, and opinion on the stock exchange itself.* For this last reason the news [as such] is often of little value, since counteracting forces [may] operate in the opposite direction.

If the wise speculator is eager to correspond with India in order to learn by way of England, Aleppo, and elsewhere, whether calm reigns there, whether the business of the Company is moving forward, whether its operations in Japan, Persia, China are proceeding favorably, whether many ships are sailing to the motherland, and whether they are richly laden,

---

* Without the "respectively," this statement could be interpreted to refer to what is now called "straddling," that is the right by the payment of a single premium to choose whether to receive or to deliver. However, there is elsewhere no clear reference to straddling; and so it seems best to regard this statement as relating to two alternative forms of contract.

† The reference here is to Ambrosio Calepino (1435–1511), Italian author of a Latin-Italian dictionary.

particularly with spices, it has been shown that, although there are difficulties, information about them all can be obtained. But even if one possesses such information, it will not be reasonable to speculate wildly in blind trust, for, if the speculator undertakes more than his [financial] strength allows and scorns Seneca's advice that the table should not be larger than the stomach, it is inevitable that he fall over with the burden and that the world slips from his shoulders, for he is no Atlas.

Even if we assume that the news is good and correct (something which one can only tentatively establish from private letters), that the reports come at the right time, and that they announce the happy arrival of the ships, nevertheless an untoward event occurring subsequent to the acquisition of the news, but before the conclusion of the business [by the Company] may destroy this splendor and contentment. For ships can sink inside of a harbor and hopes be thwarted.

But even though everything concerning India is favorable, nevertheless one would have to inform himself also about the European conditions: as to whether no disquieting naval rearmament is being undertaken, whether alliances are causing concern, and whether other (warlike) preparations could bring about a collapse of the price of the stocks. Therefore we have seen on various occasions that one portion of the speculators would buy on the strength of the Indian news, while another sells on the basis of the unclear European situation. For, in the latter case, the likelihood of [a profitable] return from the imports diminishes, while, on the other hand, costs rise [in Europe] with the raising of taxes. Even if there are wonderful means of learning the most hidden intentions of princes (apart from a case like the conquest of Babylon, which became known in the suburbs only three days afterwards), the commitments of the speculators change, and their decisions become uncertain. . . .

The difficulties and the frightful occurrences in the exchange business . . . have taught some precepts. . . . The first principle [in speculation]: *Never give anyone the advice to buy or sell shares,* because, where perspicacity is weakened, the most benevolent piece of advice can turn out badly.

The second principle: *Take every gain without showing remorse about missed profits,* because an eel may escape sooner than you think. It is wise to enjoy that which is possible without hoping for the continuance of a favorable conjuncture and the persistence of good luck.

The third principle: *Profits on the exchange are the treasures of goblins.* At one time they may be carbuncle stones, then coals, then diamonds, then flint-stones, then morning dew, then tears.

The fourth principle: *Whoever wishes to win in this game must have patience and money,* since the values are so little constant and the rumors so little founded on truth. He who knows how to endure blows without being terrified by the misfortune resembles the lion who answers the thunder with a roar, and is unlike the hind who, stunned by the thunder, tries to flee. It is certain that he who does not give up hope will win, and will secure money adequate for the operations that he envisaged at the start. Owing to the vicissitudes, many people make themselves ridiculous because some speculators are guided by dreams, others by prophecies, these by illusions, those by moods, and innumerable men by chimeras.

Merchant: People who get involved in this swindle [seem to] resemble the English Quakers who believe to contain in their bodies an inner light that advises them. [By your account] these stock-exchange people are quite silly, full of instability, insanity, pride and foolishness. They will sell without knowing the motive; they will buy without reason. They will find what is right and will err without [merit or] fault of their own. They will assume that the spirit persuades them, but the spirit [it seems] will sometimes be that of Ahab that cheats, sometimes like that of Saul that rages.

Shareholder: Your conjecture is incontestable. One speculator was dreaming of a statue of Nebuchadnezzar; whereupon he immediately sold his shares, explaining the dream: as the statue was overthrown by a pebble, so the business with

China would be lost by the Company, and, with the arrival of the Indian ships, a collapse was bound to occur. . . .

[Another] speculator enters the building of the Exchange, perplexed and not knowing which thought is misleading him or which is right. Then he has a sudden inspiration and calls out, *Vende los Kirios.** (This is an expression of the stock exchange, the meaning of which nobody understands.) He does so with no more sense than if he had observed the movement of a cloud or the passing of a hearse in the street.

Another toreador appears on the scene, earnestly trying to keep composed. He wavers as to how best to secure a profit, chews his nails, pulls his fingers, closes his eyes, takes four paces and four times talks to himself, raises his hand to his cheek as if he has a toothache, puts on a thoughtful countenance, sticks out a finger, rubs his brow, and all this accompanied by a mysterious coughing as though he could force the hand of fortune. Suddenly he rushes with violent gestures into the crowd, snaps with the fingers of one hand while with the other he makes a contemptuous gesture, and begins to deal in shares as though they were custard. He buys without restraint,[†] takes as much as he can, acquires what comes his way with no other motive or foundation than that the call of a trumpet has reached his ear. And he makes a peculiar impression when he wants to turn the circumstance to advantage, since the people on the stock exchange believe that his trumpet may cause him to commit something foolish as well as something wise.

Another eases his way into the group as though he were completely calm. Suddenly he displays excitement and starts squandering shares without any reason other than taking his coat buttons between his fingers and finding their number to be uneven. If he wins, he thinks each button a rose-bud; but, if he loses, he holds the buttons to be thorns.

---

*The Dutch version is *Verkoop de Kirien.*

[†]De la Vega uses here the phrase *a resto abierto,* after which he inserts, in a parenthesis, "which is the language of our card-sharps."

The speculators do not fail to seek protection against such excesses. They are very clever in inventing reasons for a rise in the price of the shares on occasions when there is a declining tendency, or for a fall in the midst of a boom. By "antiperistasis,"* scholars understand that the opposite has the greater power. When the air struggles with the flame, the sparks come forth with greater vehemence. . . . Because [the speculators] fear a result [opposite to that which they desire] they make greater efforts to achieve a triumph.

Sometimes a quiet state of prices is obtained and the Exchange is influenced by neither favorable nor unfavorable news. . . . Suddenly a cloud appears which portends a storm. The sellers of shares rejoice and start talk about the uncertainties in the situation and the possibilities of disasters. As quick as lightning the bulls hasten forward in order to dam the inundations and to reject this reproach on their wisdom. They resemble Aeneas who at the entrance of Hades met with a host of harpies, serpents, and centaurs, but who courageously drew his sword without being frightened and without letting anxiety paralyze his audacity. The skirmishing goes on, and at last the price is higher than before the confusion, because those groups of exchange operators who, suspecting no intrigue, had not thought of fighting and had been pursuing their regular, peaceful practices, have been awakened by the attacks. With all their strength they devote themselves to the affair and find pride in holding a weak position. Thus an obstacle becomes an advantage, and the forces which had seemed destined to throw the buyers of shares into the abyss, present them merely with an encouragement.

Despite all these absurdities, this confusion, this madness, these doubts and uncertainties of profit, means are not lacking to recognize what political or business opinions are held by persons of influence. He who makes it his business to watch these things conscientiously, without blind passion and irritating stubbornness, will hit upon the right thing innumerable

---

*From the Greek word meaning "counteraction."

times, though not always. At the conclusion of his observations, however, he will find that no perspicacity will divine the game and no science is sufficient here. For as the wealthy people [on the Exchange] also look for a counter-effect when the tendency is unfavorable, and as the indisposition of the Exchange is cured in the same way as the sufferings of a leper in Asia, . . . namely, by a poisonous medicine, . . . unfavorable news need not be regarded as fatal.

It is particularly worth remarking that in this gambling hell there are two classes of speculators who are so opposed to one another that they represent antipodes in their decisions and, as I believe, in their destinies. The first class consists of the bulls or *liefhebberen* (the latter meaning "lovers" in Flemish). They are those members of the Exchange who start their operations by purchases, just as if they were lovers of the country, of the state, and of the Company. They always desire a rise in the price of the shares; they hope that by reason of good news the market will be suddenly stirred up, and that prices will rise high rapidly. The second faction consists of the bears or the *contremine* (a name which is explained by the fact that India is considered to be a mine and that this faction strives to exhaust this mine). The bears always begin operations with sales. Some of them even surpass Timon of Athens who loved Alcibiades only in order to share his mission, namely, to be the destroyer of his native country. These bears must be fled like the plague, and one must take their part only on extraordinary occasions, as, for example, to catch a *Bichile* (which is the Dutch children's word for "butterfly"). This last is an expression used to signify a chance for a quick profit, a chance that will flutter away from you if you do not grasp it promptly, and will escape if you do not bag it quickly.

The bulls are like the giraffe which is scared by nothing, or like the magician of the Elector of Cologne, who in his mirror made the ladies appear much more beautiful than they were in reality. They love everything, they praise everything, they exaggerate everything. And as Bias deceived the ambassador of Alyattes during the siege of Priene by showing him hills of sand covered with wheat and intimating to him that such a wealthy town would never surrender because of famine, so the bulls make the public believe that their tricks signify wealth and that crops grow on graves. When attacked by serpents, they, like the Indians, regard them as both a delicate and a delicious meal. . . . They are not impressed by a fire nor perturbed by a débâcle. . . .

The bears, on the contrary, are completely ruled by fear, trepidation, and nervousness. Rabbits become elephants, brawls in a tavern become rebellions, faint shadows appear to them as signs of chaos. But if there are sheep in Africa that are supposed to serve as donkeys and wethers to serve even as horses, what is there miraculous about the likelihood that every dwarf will become a giant in the eyes of the bears? . . .

Eudicus tells that in Hestiaeotis there were two wells called Ceron and Melan and that, if the sheep drank from the first, they became white; if they drank from the second, they became black; and, if from both together, they got different colors as interesting as agreeable to the eye.* If you wish to succeed in your enterprises, don't drink continually of the well of the *liefhebberen* because it is no good to be white; but don't drink always from the well of the *contreminers* either, for it is never good to be black as a raven. . . . In short, not always Melan and not always Ceron, but always speculate for a rise from natural inclination and on a fall only on occasion, because experience has shown that usually the bulls are victorious and the bears lose out.

The Company is like the immortal tree [of mythology] which unexpectedly [and quickly] brings forth a new branch when an old one is cut off; there is no reason, therefore, [ever] to be alarmed about the Company's situation, because it overcomes every obstruction immediately by a new development.

Follow, therefore, this signpost, and press the soles of your feet into these footprints, so that the prospects may prove

---

*This story comes from Pliny's *Natural History,* bk. 31, chap. 9, who credits "Eudicus" without giving an identification or any further reference.

profitable for you, whether you act with honest or dishonest intentions. If you act with unfair intentions, there is the ordinance of Frederick Henry in case of an unfavorable turn. An honest buyer can either take delivery of the stocks or can hypothecate them; and the profit [in the transaction] is [in the end] almost certain, so that only a war (which may God forbid), and then only if it is a fierce one, could endanger the operation and intimidate us.

One has to pay attention to the different tides and to trim one's sails according to the wind. Formerly twenty speculators ruled the exchange and as the smallest circumstance had an influence, the shares fell 30 per cent because of an apprehension and 50 per cent because of a letter. Today there are as many speculators as merchants (for those playing the game merely for the sake of entertainment and not because of greediness are easily to be distinguished), and they have had sad experiences through unjustified fears. For this reason everyone watches his stocks like a jewel, and they find it extremely painful when a real loss occurs. But fearing a mere menace means to experience grief and sorrow twice, and in advance of reality. . . .

A high price of shares causes concern to many who are not accustomed to it. But reasonable men need not be disturbed about the matter, since every day the position of the [East India] Company becomes more splendid, the state wealthier, and the revenue from investments at fixed interest becomes less, inasmuch as it is difficult to find ways of investing money. The rate of interest on ordinary loans amounts to only 3 per cent a year, and, if the creditor receives security, to only 2½ per cent. Therefore, even the wealthiest men are forced to buy stocks, and there are people who do not sell them when the prices have fallen, in order to avoid a loss. But they do not sell at rising prices either [to protect a gain], because they do not know a more secure investment for their capital. Moreover, in this kind of investment, their funds can be recovered in the quickest [possible] way, since with an active state of [stock-exchange] business one can always have control of his money.

The possibility of quick sales increases the value of the stocks in such a manner that the shares of the Amsterdam chamber command a higher price than those of all other chambers.* This happens only because speculation does not exist at the other places in these Provinces. The dividends, apart from small expenses, are the same for the outside chambers; yet the shares of the chamber of Zeeland are quoted 150 per cent, of Enkhuysen 80 per cent, of Hoorn 75 per cent, of Rotterdam 30 per cent, of Delft 70 per cent less than the shares of the Amsterdam chamber.

The variations of the price [of the stock in Amsterdam] do not [necessarily] follow the course of the river Moelin which runs toward the East for one fortnight and then toward the West for another. Neither is there a similarity to the Persian well in which the water rose for thirty years and fell for a similar period. The fall of prices need not have a limit, and there are also unlimited possibilities for the rise. When a merchant bought a diamond of immeasurable value at Goa and brought it from India to Europe, he was scolded by the French king who asked him, "How could you risk a whole fortune on this stone?" The wise and polite answer was: "I simply had Your Majesty in mind all the time." Therefore the excessively high values need not alarm you. There never lack princes of the exchange and kings of manipulations who are enamored of the shares. Be aware of the fact that there are as many speculators as there are people, and that there will always be buyers who will free you from anxiety. . . .

The expectation of an event creates a much deeper impression upon the exchange than the event itself. When large dividends or rich imports are expected, shares will rise in price; but if the expectation becomes a reality, the shares often fall; for the joy over the favorable development and the jubilation over a lucky chance have abated in the meantime. There are natural reasons for this phenomenon. Whenever the situation is threatening, the bears generally fear the blow, and they do not dare to engage themselves. Meanwhile, the bulls are

---

*The shareholders located in the several Dutch cities were constituted into "chambers" and as such participated in the governing of the Company through the choice of officers. Shares represented in one chamber could not be transferred to another.

optimistic with joy over the state of business affairs, which is steadily favorable to them; and their attitude is so full of [unthinking] confidence that even less favorable news does not impress them and causes no anxiety. But as soon as the ships arrive or the dividends are declared, the sellers take new courage. They calculate that for some months the purchasers—the bulls—will not be able to expect very propitious [new] events. So the leaves tremble in the softest breeze, and the smallest shadow causes fear—and therefore no wonder that the shares fall, because they are abandoned by the one side and are attacked by the other. Clever people make skillful use of advantages that are offered by destiny . . . ; for, if a sudden change takes place, [the speculators] can hardly pull their feet [out of the fire], and when in great difficulties they can at best save their limbs. . . .

Merchant: [As I gather from your description], the terms used on the Exchange are not carefully chosen. I notice that the language there is Arabic grafted upon Greek, and that even the most experienced person needs a new dictionary to understand it. . . . There is no expression which is not as incomprehensible as God. I really thought that I was at the construction of the Tower of Babel when I heard the confusion of tongues and the mixture of languages on the stock exchange. Sometimes they used Latin words such as *opsie,* sometimes Dutch ones such as *bichile,* and sometimes French ones such as *surplus.**

Shareholder: As to the confusion of tongues on the Exchange, I am not to be blamed for it. The jargon was coined by the necessities of the business, then became customary and proved to be practical. I sell the phrases at cost price and profit nothing save the effort to bring them forward and to explain them. . . .

Philosopher: [Going back to practices on the Exchange, I have a question. You allege that when,] because of the arrival

---

*The word "surplus" was employed to mean the difference in values at the settlement of contracts.

of unexpected news, those who think it propitious buy, and the others who judge it less favorable sell, it is considered particularly wise [for the novice or the doubter] to talk to the purchasers and to converse with the sellers, to weigh opinions and reasons, and to take the most advantageous course after these efforts, [in order] to do the most promising sort of business. [This contradicts propriety.] I would like to ask whether the speculators are obliged to inform me of their secrets, or whether a speculation may be based upon the hope of such a communication. When you yourself note that a fortunate opportunity is missed in the blinking of an eye, how can it be reasonable to lose time with conversations? . . .

[But, before you answer that question, let me make a few additional comments. For example, it seems] incompatible with philosophy that the bears should sell after the reason for their sales has ceased to exist, since the philosophers teach that when the cause ceases, the effect ceases also. But if the bears obstinately go on selling, there is an effect even after the cause had disappeared. Moreover, while philosophy teaches that different effects are ascribable to different causes, . . . at the stock exchange some buy and some sell on the basis of a given piece of news, so that here one cause has different effects. . . .

However, there are other activities [of the stock exchange] . . . which do not contradict my philosophy. One such action is the strong resistance offered by the bulls against the attacks of the bears, which you have so well described. The result is that the shares rise even during the greatest danger. . . . Nor am I surprised that both parties fight with words, with hands and with feet, with mental exertion, and at the risk of their fortunes. . . . [Given the situation, I suppose that I should not be] surprised that some speculators consider a certain piece of news favorable, others unfavorable. Facts are changed by emotions, and they appear to each person in a different light. . . .

Your advice to do little business meets with my approbation; its suits my temperament. Moreover, philosophy teaches . . . that the stomach cannot digest an excess of food, . . . and [accordingly] it is very sensible to be satisfied with [limited] profits, even if one does not gain all [possible] riches and advantages. . . . At the stock exchange the speculators call a failure a slap in the face. I consider him a fool who exposes himself to such slaps. . . .

Finally, I assure you that my inclination is always directed toward a rise of prices, although I will talk to the bears. They are always pessimists, and I want to keep free from biases in the heat of the battle.

Shareholder: I had decided to translate these dialogues into French so that knowledge of the stock exchange, about which nobody has written so far,* might become general. As I realized that many passages which were based on puns could not be translated, I thought it proper to add anecdotes and embroidery, and to round off both erudition and deep thoughts with an elegant and harmonious presentation. . . .

Since the jokes at the Exchange, in so far as they are not objectionable, form a main attraction to the business, it is not out of place to mention the innuendos in a description of the Exchange. I do not wish to give offense, I only report or, to put it better, I shoot into the air, for, as the attacks cannot then be directed toward individual persons, the arrow will not hit any particular mark.

I have promised to give a truthful account and I could not do this without an exact reproduction of the facts. And when severe critics reply that the truth is not violated by those who hide it, but by those who alter it, I assure you that I should not suppress the slightest detail I know of. I am, therefore, faithful to this obligation in so far as I do not consider the matters indecent. . . .

---

*Pringsheim in his introduction to the German translation of de la Vega states, "This assertion of the author is not quite correct, as a few pamphlets treating of the speculation in shares were published in 1642 and 1687. The author either does not know them at all, or makes no mention of them because he thinks them too irrelevant." *Die Verwirrung der Verwirrungen* . . . , p. 89.

Third Dialogue

Shareholder: Among the plays which men perform in taking different parts in this magnificent world theatre, the greatest comedy is played at the Exchange. There, in an inimitable fashion, the speculators excel in tricks, they do business and find excuses wherein hiding-places, concealment of facts, quarrels, provocations, mockery, idle talk, violent desires, collusion, artful deceptions, betrayals, cheatings, and even the tragic end are to be found. In a song Horace extols the sweet ecstasy of a fool who fancied himself always sitting in a wonderful theatre where the actors entertained him, and the intricacy of the play filled him with delight:

> *Qui se credebat miros audire tragedo*
> *In vacuo laetus sessor, plausoque theatro.**

There is nothing more entertaining than to hear the comedies that can pass as a symbol of the genius of academicians.

Thus the whole stock exchange is represented in the drama "The palace in confusion," the bulls in "Much sufferings for much profit," the bears in "The wild beast, the flash of lightning, and the stone," the uninterested in "The game is an affair of fools," the skillful gamblers in "There is no life but honor"; the Fredericks are represented in "Fortune and misfortune of the name," the lucky speculators in "May God's Son grant you fortune," the unlucky ones in "Defiance of destiny." Finally I should like you to play "The eye-opener," though I am about to perform "Give all and give nothing," for, although I teach you carefully all I know, I am convinced that I give you nothing when I want to give you everything.†

---

* This couplet is taken from Horace's *Epistulae,* II, 2, 129.

† De la Vega may here be citing actual Spanish plays. At any rate, the first five can be identified as probably *El palacio confuso* by Antonio Mira de Amescua (1570-1640), *Sulfrir por querer mas* by Geronomo de Villayzán (1604-1633), *La fiera, el rayo y la piedra* by Pedro Calderon de la Barca (1600-1681), *Entre bobos anda el juego* by Francisco de Rojas y Zorilla (1607-1648), and *No hay vida como la honra* by Juan Perez de Montalban (1602-1638).

Philosopher: Then I shall perform "What happened one night,"* for last night my peace was turned into unrest, my calmness into despair, my awe into mockery, my knowledge into ignorance, my equanimity into frenzy, my respect into abuse. A speculator cheated me; a cheater took me at my word; a betrayer stole my reputation.

There happened to be a few friends who talked of shares and gave the prevailing price as 576. To the timid they declared that the figure was excessive, and to the courageous that it was moderate. I was pleased to hear the confirmation of my opinion and, as I well remembered the advice to speculate on a rise and as I wanted to support the faction which loves the country and the Company, I sought to demonstrate my opinion by bidding 586 for a share to a bear, who was proclaiming the ruin of the state. Hardly had I made the bid, when I was told just as quickly as excitedly that the share was mine. So great was the noise, the shouting, and the laughter in which the other players indulged because of my audacity and their anxiety, that I blushed, not because of my foolishness, but from fury and shame.

The whole night I passed restlessly, thinking that they had taken money out of my purse. This morning at dawn I inquired about the value of this paper, when a scoundrel informed me (I don't know if with seriousness or merely in order to torture me) that the price stood at [5]64 and would sink very soon to [5]20. It was a miracle that I did not fall down dead or at least in a faint. . . .

Merchant: The rogues maintained that we [must have] been bitten by the tarantula [because we were so excited] and turned the conversation to the matter of "opsies".† They found me full of resentment, because of the vexations that they had caused our philosopher [friend], and, driven by anger, I asked

---

*Antonio Coello (1600-1653) wrote a play by this name, the Spanish title reading *Lo que pasa en una noche.*

†The merchant's use of the pronoun "we" suggests that he was a member of the group—the "few friends"—with whom the philosopher had forgathered the previous evening.

how high would be the amount of the premium for delivery at [5]80 in October. One of the rogues retorted cunningly that he would not bind himself to any rate, but would estimate the premium as 20 per cent. I offered him 15 per cent, whereupon he accepted my proposition with the remark that he would take the risk as a favor to me. And whereas I was at the time grateful for this courtesy, I was informed today that the premium amounted to 9 [per cent] at most.

In spite of all this unpleasantness, however, I console myself that I did not fall from such a high roof as our friend [the philosopher], for I know what I can lose, and the difference is no more than 6 per cent; whereas he suffers already a loss of 10 per cent, without knowing how great this loss can become and how long his uncertainty may last.*

Shareholder: Lest you should plume yourself too boastfully, I wish to tell you that he can be freed from distress sooner than you from anger. It is an inviolable practice on the Exchange (which once was a mere usance) that the party making a mistake is not obligated to suffer for it, if a transaction, not done at the price of the day, contains an error of 10 per cent [of the par value]. In case of unexpected news, unscrupulous traders may make offers over or under the price [of the day] and try to attract buyers or sellers by this means. It is, however, necessary to get an acknowledgment of the transaction, even if it is not advantageous [for the swindler] to give the acknowledgement, as soon as the opposite party has found himself in the error. Although the reaction of the market is [in fact] quite varied in the face of unforeseen news, practice has introduced the foregoing definite rule. Therefore, [the philosopher] can not only not be forced to take the stocks at more than 576 but he can also refuse to carry out the transaction at all. And besides since it is his first operation and because it is generally

---

*The argument here seems to relate to the amount of loss deriving from the follies in the respective cases. The philosopher paid 586 for stock when its market price was only 576; so he had an initial (paper) loss of 10 points. On the other hand, the merchant submitted to a 15 per cent premium when he might have gotten one of 9 per cent; so he stood to lose 6 points by reason of his ignorance or carelessness.

known that he is no businessman, it is easy to negate the offer and to prevent the loss. . . .

[To be sure, there is widespread honesty and expedition on the Exchange. For example,] the business in stocks and the bustle of the sales which are made when unforeseen news arrives is wonderful to behold. Nobody changes the decisions which he makes in his momentary passion, and his words are held sacred even in the case of a price difference of 50 per cent; and, although tremendous business is done by the merchants without the mediation of brokers who could serve as witnesses, no confusion occurs and no quarrels take place. . . .

Such honesty, co-operation, and accuracy are admirable and surprising. But to make payments for obligations which according to the Exchange usances do not exist, when your credit is not endangered and your reputation not likely to suffer,—that is not liberality, but insanity; it is not punctuality, but prodigality; not courage, but the foolishness of Don Quixote. . . .

The Exchange business is comparable to a game. Some of the players behave like princes and combine strength with tenderness and amiability with intelligence, but there are some participants who lose their reputation and others who lack devotion to their business even before the play begins.

A witty man, observing the business on the Exchange, the studied impoliteness there, remarked that the gamble on the Exchange was like death in that it made all people equal. . . .

[I would also remark that] a twenty per cent drop in the stock prices is not large enough to be considered a serious blow. . . . You do not have to despair and to bemoan your fate, for, as the price may drop twenty per cent over-night, it may also rise fifty per cent in the same period. . . .

[However, one had best never get involved in stock speculation.] It is a great error to assume that you can withdraw [temporarily] from the Exchange or that you can gain peace of mind when you cease to meet with the other speculators. If ill fate pursues you persistently, it can reach you just as well in the rocks and the forests, where lightning may strike you and wild beasts may attack you. . . . Moreover, it is foolish to think that you can withdraw from the Exchange after you have tasted [the sweetness of the honey]. . . . He who has [once] entered the [charmed] circle of the Exchange is in eternal agitation and sits in a prison, the key of which lies in the ocean and the bars of which are never opened. . . .

Merchant: I suppress my objections [to some of your ideas] . . . and ask you only for an explanation of the meaning of "West" and "East".

Shareholder: "East" and "West" are abbreviated Dutch terms; and whereas the "Company" we have talked about till now is called the "Company of the East" because of its undertakings in East India, there is also another company, called the "Company of the West", whose field of activities lies in the West Indies.

The founding of this latter Company took place in 1621, and the capital amounted to between 120 and 130 tons of gold. Its trade took such an admirable upswing that the shares of West and East reached the same value, and it seemed as if the West Indian shares would become a precious treasure. But fortune changed. The cloves were lost, Brazil broke away, fortune and prosperity vanished, splendor and reputation suffered, and opinion changed so greatly that the shares were sold at $3\frac{1}{8}$ per cent, and the sellers feared a still greater loss.

In 1674 the *Bewinthebberen* (a title which in Dutch means "directors" and is used in both Companies) proposed a reorganization of the Company in order to repair the damage and to avoid the impending ruin, [a reorganization] through which the endangered capital would be increased by contributions from the interested parties. This kind of aid was called a *Bijlegh,* and those who disapproved of the reorganization could be forced by order of the legal authorities to sell their shares; but a compromise was permitted: the shares could be transferred to the other chambers upon payment of a small transfer charge.

The Company had three kinds of obligations: first, there were the obligations toward the shareholders, whether the shares had been inherited from the original subscribers or had been purchased; secondly, the owners of deposits had to be satisfied, men who had left money with the Company at low interest and who, as wealthy people, were satisfied with this return of interest; thirdly, there were the outstanding bottomries or sea loans which had been taken in order to extend the trade.

In the reorganization the shareholders had to pay in 4 per cent in cash, and they were paid in new shares 15 per cent of the nominal value of the old shares. The owners of deposits had to add 8 per cent, and in return received in [new] shares 30 per cent of the nominal value of their claims. Of the sea loans, the old ones were differentiated with the new. In the case of the old ones 30 per cent in shares were given in return for cash payment of 8 per cent, while [the owners of] the more recent loans received 50 per cent in cash and 50 per cent in shares without deduction.

This reorganization was carried through at the cost of 70 tons of gold, and it was after due consideration that the distinctions mentioned above were made. It was just that the shareholders be favored least, because they had been interested in both profit and loss of the Company; but the owners of deposits were allowed to suffer a smaller loss of their more liquid claim, for they had only demanded a moderate interest and were excluded from gain or loss. Nevertheless, the bottomry loans were treated even more favorably, because they were of more recent date than the deposits. For this same reason a distinction was also made between the older and newer claims, as we have just reported.

As a result of these operations the Company took on new life. (There have been, however, so few distributions of profits during the last fourteen years that the total dividend amounts to no more than 26 per cent.) The price of the shares holds at 110 per cent from the hope that large return cargoes will arrive from Guinea and Caraçao. Though the contract [now to be mentioned] offers shortcomings too, people believe in a brilliant development of the business.

The contract in question (upon which are based the most important [current] undertakings of the Company), consists in the obligation of a few Dutch merchants to take at a fixed price in Curaçao as many Negroes as the Company is able to carry from the coast of Guinea. As the merchants sell the slaves again to the [Spanish] West Indies, they gain no less by this stipulation than the Company—in a business for the running of which [incidentally] an agent is stationed in Spain and on behalf of which a duty is paid to the king.

This arrangement provides the main basis of speculation in these shares, [the prices] of which could be unfavorably influenced by [political] complications in Europe because of the increased risk to the shipments and because of the disadvantage in the [then unavoidable] increase of taxes. . . .

[I should add that] although each company is interested in peace and in the security of the state, particular factors exist which affect the two varieties of shares differently and cause them either to rise or fall [without reference to one another]. In addition certain groups have been formed. (They are generally called "Cabalas." I do not know whether this name is derived from *cabal** or from *cabiloso.*†) Through the manoeuvres of these rings, it is possible for owners of East shares to be freed from their engagements in order to strengthen their position in "West", and vice versa. If the stock exchange turns away from one variety of share in order to favor the other, and if many shares of one kind are sold against cash in order to push up the price of the other, either by purchasing the other stock outright or by loaning to other speculators through hypothecation of *their* purchases, the speculators fear a sudden fall [in the price of the first stock], and they become depressed from fear of further attacks. Therefore they speed up their sales [of this second stock]; the zest for this paper diminishes, and its price falls.

These [West] shares are not traded on the basis of 500 pounds (nominal value) as are those of the "East," but on that of 1,000 pounds. . . . [To be sure,] they were for a short time dealt in at 500 pounds although their value, if not the risk in trading in them, was much less [than in the case of East]. But certain greedy merchants demanded that the brokerage fee be cut in half (it amounted for each party to only 1½ gulden per

---

*The Spanish word meaning "complete."

†The Spanish word meaning "one who enters into intrigues."

share instead of 3 gulden for "East") and the brokers countered with a requirement that each contract should amount to at least 1,000 pounds in order to earn 6 gulden for the same amount of work. Though the fee seems at first sight to be great, not with relation to the value of the shares but with that of the facility of the contracting, so great is the loyalty of some brokers to their principals, whom they usually call their masters, and so great is their industry, their activity, their zeal, and their vigilance that the customers get their money's worth, even with the [admittedly] moderate honesty of the brokers.

But since in this business the same tricks are usual as in the trade with "East" and since the trading in these shares is equally honest and equally fraudulent, we will continue to concern ourselves with the tricks of the first line of business, which is the most common in this city and the best known around the world. . . .

Merchant: If it is not too great a trouble for our friend, I should like to hear also about the place and the ways of the exchange transactions, how business is done, for, although we know the origin, the innovators, and the confusions of the stock exchange, we do not yet know anything about the kind of business dealings or about the site of the contest.

Shareholder: The business is so constant and incessant that hardly a definite place can be named where it goes on. The Dam and the Exchange, however, are the places most frequented. On the Dam, business is done from ten to twelve a.m., at the Exchange from twelve to two p.m.

The Dam is a square which is faced by The Palace [i.e., the town hall]. In Dutch *Dam* means a dyke against the floods, for at this place once a dyke had been constructed in order to protect the town against the Amstel, the river from which the town got its name, as Amsterdam was originally called Amstel Dam.

Here on this square the game begins in the morning. It lasts until the gates of the Exchange are closed at noon.* Then the crowds gather in great haste in order not to be fined for coming late. Thereafter the struggle is carried on at the

---

* "Closed" in this connection meant open only on payment of a fine.

Exchange; and even from the greatest exhaustion the weapons are not laid down and during the great excitement no recuperation is allowed.

The Exchange is an enclosed building surrounded by columns. (Some people lean against these columns of the Exchange which [they find to be] like columns of fire, others hide behind them as behind a cloud.) The name "Exchange" is explained by the fact that it encloses the merchants like a purse or because here everybody makes eager efforts to fill his purse. As the word "purse" means skin in Greek, [perhaps not surprisingly] it is that many players leave their skins at the Exchange. . . .

The way in which the transactions [on the Exchange] are concluded is as ridiculous as the game itself. In the Levant an agreement is made by nodding the head. Here, however, handshakes or hand-slaps are the signs of agreement. But how painful! Many strive for the victory which the blows of the hands promise and they have only to lament the blows of fate. . . .

A member of the Exchange opens his hand and another takes it, and thus sells a number of shares at a fixed price, which is confirmed by a second handshake. With a new handshake a further item is offered, and then there follows a bid. The hands redden from the blows (I believe from the shame that even the most respected people do business in such an indecent manner as with blows). The handshakes are followed by shouting, the shouting by insults, the insults by impudence and more insults, shouting, pushes, and handshakes until the business is finished. In Holy Scripture I read that one clapped one's hands in surprise as well as on festive occasions. Here [at the Exchange], however, they clap their hands together for joy as well as in surprise. . . . Some applaud the cheating; others wring their hands in surprise at the losses. They applaud as at a comedy, and they wring their hands in astonishment at the ruin [of their hopes]. . . .

[The philosopher interrupts to compare the shareholder's vivid description with classical paintings. Whereupon the shareholder continues:]

In order to obtain even greater applause for my presentation, I wish to describe the nervous condition of the speculators and the restlessness of their behavior at their business. I think that they have undoubtedly been given the name *actionists* because they are always in action. . . . Thoughts about their own activities have impressed themselves so much on their fantasies that [it is alleged] they deal, act, and quarrel while sleeping.

Two of my friends slept together. The one struck the other on the head which caused a swelling. When the latter wakened his friend with shouts, he assured his companion that he had just concluded a transaction by that blow. This speculator was a second Pythagoras; the latter was wakened by a cock, the speculator by a bump, and in Portuguese both are called "gallo". . . .

When the speculators talk, they talk shares; when they run an errand, the shares make them do so; when they stand still, the shares act like a rein; when they look at something, it is shares that they see; when they think hard, the shares provide the content of their thoughts; if they eat, the shares are their food; if they meditate or study, they think of the shares; in their fever fantasies, they are occupied with shares; and even on the death bed, their last worries are the shares. . . .

But what surpasses all these enormities . . . and what is hardly believable (because it seems to be complete fancy rather than over-exaggeration) is the fact that the speculator fights his own good sense, struggles against his own will, counteracts his own hope, acts against his own comfort, and is at odds with his own decisions. . . . There are many occasions in which every speculator seems to have two bodies so that astonished observers see a human being fighting himself. If, for example, there arrives a piece of news which would induce the speculator to buy, while the atmosphere prevailing at the stock exchange forces him to sell, his reasoning fights his own good reasons. At one moment his reasoning drives him to buy, because of the information that has just arrived; at the other it induces him to sell because of the trend at the Exchange.

Merchant: We are informed about the manner, the place, and now the restless nature of the Exchange activities. Still I wish to know how the Exchange transactions are wound up, how the shares are transferred and paid for.

Shareholder: I have already told you of the three classes which take part in the Exchange. The first is constituted of the large capitalists or the princes of the Exchange, the second of the merchants, and the third of the professional speculators.

The capitalists who live on the interest of a princely fortune preserve the dignity of princes in this business. In order to avoid all the troubles connected with the transactions, they never visit the Exchange themselves, but give the orders which they think advantageous, to the broker who carries them out as best he can. Sometimes, when a decided trend prevails, it is possible to execute an order with the greatest promptness. But there are also cases where crafty men sense the direction of his purpose and inject such confusion into his operations that he can execute the order only with [unanticipated] disadvantage and difficulty.

Some of the merchants, like the great financiers, do not visit the Exchange themselves but also give their orders to brokers. They do not think it appropriate to allow themselves to be upset by attacks, insults, and shouts. In order to escape all this unpleasantness, they avoid the crowds on the Exchange. There are, however, other merchants who go to the Exchange daily (as do the speculators); and there are five reasons why, in doing so, they manifest a preference of advantage over respectability and of profit over propriety. First, they do not wish to pay brokerage fees, and so they do business directly with other merchants of their own circle, a procedure which saves them trouble and work. Secondly, they like to have the pleasure of the hand-shakes, for they are [cordial] people who are glad to take a hand and who make efforts to reach out their hands. Thirdly, [if they decide to use a broker,] they have the advantage of personal contact with him—a circumstance that gives them always an advantage of a half per cent more than his broker would offer a fellow broker. This is done because the broker considers the merchants to be reliable customers, whereas he does not know [even] whether he himself is thought absolutely reliable by the other broker. Again, when dealing with the latter he would receive only half of the brokerage fee, but he receives the fee from both parties at the same time when he arranges a transaction with a merchant. Fourthly, the merchants visit the Exchange to learn about the trend of values, whether prices are rising or falling. And as the whole stock exchange crowds round these influential men in order to execute the transactions initiated by them, it is very easy for the merchants to divine the intentions [of other operators], to check the news minutely, and thus to obtain advantage from the contacts. Fifthly, they believe that their minds will sense the best possibilities, because they are *virtuosi* and veterans of business and because nobody will be able to exercise better skill than they themselves.

"Look after that which concerns you" is the advice of a prudent man. People efficient in business follow this counsel, because they believe that nobody will care better for their advantage than they themselves, and that nobody will better grab hold of fortune than they themselves can. . . .

I am not surprised that there are speculators who, though free from avarice, do not give their orders to persons—the brokers—who would doubtlessly carry them out just as eagerly as honestly, and just as honestly as punctually. But what I complain of is that some such speculators, operating under the pretext of trying to please a broker, are friendly with him (without really intending to be of real advantage to the latter). They give him an order to buy one or several shares, but at the moment of execution they appear on the Exchange themselves and offer a higher rate than they had authorized the unfortunate broker to bid, whom they had thus deceived by cajolery. What is the use of giving an order, if in the same moment means are sought to prevent its execution? Is it not obvious that in case of a higher offer the shares are more likely to be delivered to the speculators themselves than to the broker . . . whom they have treated just as smilingly as falsely and just as deceitfully as cordially? . . .

We have already stated that there are three kinds of dealings in shares. But you should also appreciate that three ways of settlement are possible. First of all there are direct transfers. For their execution, the seller of the shares has to go to the offices of the Company, located in its magnificent building, and there he is required to have the stock transferred to the account of the buyer or of the lender. (As noted, earlier, even the wealthiest people make use of this hypothecation of shares without endangering their credit.) After the sum has been paid in bank money, the officials of the Bank certify that the payment has been made correctly (the whole procedure being what we call turning "a share into cash").* This is done with greater or less care according to the hurry of the buyer or the need of the seller for his money,—and complaints are sometimes made of the haste and sometimes of the carelessness displayed in the operations.

The second kind of Exchange business is done *on days of settlement.* By this one understands (or ought to at least) that the stocks are to be taken up on the twentieth of the month in which the transactions [in question] have taken place, and that they are to be paid for on the twenty-fifth of the same month. But negligence, disorder, and confusion have gained ground in this settlement process, for one neither takes delivery nor pays when one should. There are brokers whom we call *rescounters,* since they make it their business to balance out or rescounter the commitments and to pay and to receive the *differences* [only]. And as there are some among these men too who seek profit in procrastination and obscurities, it is necessary in dealing with them to watch over one's advantage and interests rather than try to be polite and courteous.

The third kind of transaction takes place *at later dates* still. Here the shares must be delivered and be paid for on the twentieth and twenty-fifth of the month which is specified in the contract, unless one makes use of the mysterious prolongations of which I disapprove because they damage the credit and endanger the reputation [of the party who asks for the prolongation]. For these time bargains the brokers use printed *contract forms* with the customary stipulations and conditions of the business. On these forms spaces are left only for the names, dates, and prices. When two copies have been filled out and signed, the

---

*See Pringsheim's introduction to the German translation, p. 135.

contracts are exchanged by the two parties; [later,] and after the establishment of the profit or loss in the business by the rescounters, they are re-exchanged by the signatories.

For the *option business* there exists another sort of *contract form,* from which it is evident when and where the premium was paid and of what kind are the signatories' obligations. The *forms for hypothecating* are different also. Stamped paper is used for them, upon which regulations concerning the *dividends* and other details are set down, so that there can be no doubt and no disagreement regarding the arrangements.

As to the unactionable feature of any speculative transaction to be settled by the payment of differences, you are right in remarking that with *cash transactions* the regulation lacks pertinence.* It is, however, valid in the case of *time bargains* unless the seller has the shares transferred to the time account of the purchaser within a fortnight. Then the buyer is obliged to take up the shares, or declare himself insolvent.

Though the opinion prevails generally that this regulation does not apply in the case of the seller but only in that of the buyer, this is an error introduced by bad practice. The lawyers assert that the seller as well as the buyer is allowed to raise the objection [envisaged by Frederick Henry's edict].

The public also presumes that, if the seller of stocks buys them back (from someone who had purchased them earlier), the law does not apply. That is undoubtedly an error also. (For instance), the edict does not apply when I buy a share at [5] 40, sell it at [5] 20, and declare before witnesses that the stock so sold will serve to settle the account of shares previously purchased. By this action I have declared myself debtor for the difference of 20 per cent [of the face value] which I have lost. Therefore I am not permitted to appeal to the regulation, since I have already assumed a debt; I must pay the difference or become insolvent. But if I have bought a share at 40 from someone and without subsequent declaration I sell him another

---

* "Regulation" in the ensuing passage refers to the edict of Frederick Henry. See Introduction, p. viii.

share at 20, [the seller in neither case really owning the stock,] I need neither declare myself bankrupt in order to free myself [from the obligation in question] nor disappear in order to shake loose; [I can merely appeal to the edict].

As to whether the regulation is applicable to *option contracts,* the opinions of experts diverge widely. I have not found any decision that might serve as a precedent, though there are many cases at law from which one [should be able to] draw a correct picture. All legal experts hold that the regulation is applicable to both the seller and the buyer [of the contract]. In practice, however, the judges have often decided differently, always freeing the buyer from the liability while often holding the seller [to the contract]. (If the assumption is true that the regulation applies to both seller and purchaser), I can rely on it if [as a trader] I have received call premiums and am forced to deliver the stocks on the day of settlement, or if, as a receiver of a put premium, I have to take shares on the day of settlement. If, on the contrary, the opinion is correct that it applies only to the seller, the regulation will be of no use to me [as a person wanting to seek shelter] when I receive call premiums, for in this case I am in fact a seller; but it will help me if I have received a put premium, as I am then the buyer of stocks. With regard to the put premium, however, there are also great differences of opinion, for, while the scholars assume that no [legally valid] claims can be made because of the regulation, there are contrary decisions by the courts, so that law and legal opinion, the regulation and the reasons for the decisions are contradictory. The theory remains uncertain, and one cannot tell which way the adjudication tends.

However, if the payer of a put premium possesses the stocks on the day of the negotiation of the contract so that he could offer to make delivery to me and to have them transferred to my account [within] a fortnight after the offer, it is unlikely that in such a situation, embarrassing though it might be to me, the regulation can be appealed to. According to the opinion of some people, it is sufficient if the payer of the premium possesses the shares on the day when he declares [himself ready to make] the delivery and not already on the day when he entered into the premium contract, in order to make all objections on grounds of the regulation ineffective.

The same uncertainty of adjudication exists with respect to the hypothecation of stocks. While it is generally assumed that, if the shares fall below the value used as the basis of the loan, the mortgagee is obliged to pay in the difference or declare himself insolvent, a few very speculative minds have argued (uncertain doubtless because of the paucity of facts to sustain their position) that if the shares have not been transferred to the time account which I as money lender maintain, within a fortnight after the start of the hypothecation arrangement, and if the shares remain in the account [of the borrower] until the date of payment [of the loan], I can raise objections [under the regulation] in order to garner a profit as well as to save myself from a possible loss.*

The most amusing thing and the height of fun is the view of two brokers who peck at each other around a piece of business, for under such conditions every respect for the customer disappears, all inhibitions are gone, their voices grow more impudent, their insults more vigorous, and their handshakes more ridiculous. The one broker offers 500 pounds and the other accepts [the proposition] (which is called *Serpilladas*† in the language of the Exchange), or the one broker bids a specific price for the shares, whereupon the other retorts furiously, "They are yours" (which in the exchange language means "to be captured"). Whether the shares are "captured" or "stolen," the surrounding Exchange people quarrel with one another, and the inquisitive folk make such a noise that an abyss seems to open and the Furies appear to be fighting. . . .

There are two kinds of brokers. Some are appointed by the municipal authorities and are called "sworn" brokers, for they

---

* De la Vega seems to be arguing on the basis of a legal figment: because the value of the collateral had fallen below that on which the loan had been calculated, the borrower, still holding on to the shares, was involved in borrowing on a fictitious basis—and so resembling the short seller, the receiver of a call premium who really didn't have stock to deliver, &c.

† The Spanish words *ser pilladas* mean "to be taken away" or "to be packed off."

take an oath not to do business on their own account. Their number is limited, and it changes only in the case of death or through special privilege, which is seldom conferred. The other class of brokers is called "free" brokers, also "drones" . . . , in order to indicate that they snatch the honey, their profits, from the other brokers. If the free brokers were to be sued, they would have to pay a fine for impairing the income [of the sworn brokers]; but such action is taken only in cases of personal revenge, otherwise clemency and indulgence toward these brokers prevail, instead of the sworn brokers attending actively to their own interests.

There exists an infinite number of these free brokers. This occupation is [in many cases] the only recourse for impoverished [businessmen], and the best place of refuge for many ruined careers. The stock business is so lively and widespread that, though there are innumerable free brokers, they all earn a living and they need neither become robbers who eat in order to kill, nor hunters who kill in order to eat. They all live, they all make progress, they all distinguish themselves and try to substitute great activity for lack of an official appointment. They appear so faithful and concerned about their customers that they compensate by zeal what they lack in reputation, and by devotion to business for what they lack in [tangible wealth to give] security. . . .

Philosopher: [There is still another stock-exchange matter of which you have as yet made no mention.] Those wretches who on that fateful night brought me to distress, spoke of *ducaton shares,* and I will not be satisfied until you explain to me the meaning of that term.

Shareholder: Some clerks have discovered that the speculation in ordinary shares (which are called *large* or *paid-up shares*) was too hazardous for their slight resources. They began, therefore, a less daring game in which they dealt in small shares. For while with whole shares one could win or lose 30 gulden of Bank money for every point that the price rose or fell, with the small shares one risked only a ducaton [3 gulden] for each point. The new speculation, called trading in *ducaton shares,* began in 1683. For a simple mode of clearing the transactions, the aid of a man who was called the General Cashier was secured. This man put down all contracts in a book, although previously only oral agreements had existed. For every contract that was put down, the General Cashier got a *placa* from each party.* Before the transactions were booked definitively, the cashier communicated with the two parties. One rarely agrees in this business to a transaction with a longer time to run than one month, because the resources of the people concerned are not sufficient. On the first day of each month when the clock of the Exchange shows one-thirty p.m., the cashier is told the price of the large shares by two impartial stock-exchange men and, in accordance with these statements, he specifies the value of the small shares. This comedy is called "raising the stick," because formerly a stick was raised by the cashier, until this custom was given up because of the noise that was made each time. The fixing of the price is followed by the settlement of the transactions (in so far as they have not been settled in the middle of the month). Payment is made in cash, and is more punctual than with the large shares, so that even the most experienced businessmen take part in this trade in small shares, for, tempted by the punctuality, they overlook the dubious reputation of the business and endorse it [by their actions].

This branch of trade has been increasing during the last five years to such an extent (and mainly with a certain group which is as boisterous as it is quick-witted) that it is engaged in by both sexes, old men, women, and children. . . . Therefore, the means devised to reduce hazards has in fact made the dangers more widespread. The speculation has been so extended that one deals in whole regiments of [ducaton] shares, as if they were matches, and I fear that some day those concerned in the business will be burnt and ruined. . . .†

When a mirror is broken, each piece of crystal remains a mirror, the only difference being that the small mirrors reflect one's countenance in miniature and the large ones in larger

---

* *Placa* is the Spanish word for the small coin called a *stuiver* by the Dutch.

† Cf. below, regarding the abandonment of this type of speculation in 1688, p. 40.

size. . . . Stock shares are similar to mirrors, at least a special sort of mirror which makes it appear that the reflected object is hanging in mid-air, or that sort that makes the viewers stiffen from amazement because, while they are looking, they see themselves flying by. Or they are like the mirror of Achaia which, when swung back and forth over a fountain, predicted for one person life and for another death. Fearful persons broke this mirror [the large "East" shares] and cut the crystal into pieces by agreeing to regard each 500 pounds of the large shares as 5,000 small ones. They intended thereby to moderate the trade, but they managed merely to make many transactions out of one, and from one mirror many. . . .

The reason why nearly all of the [speculators] participate so eagerly in the trading in small shares is the intention of the buyers of large shares to sell them as small ones, (because at the beginning of the month the price of the small shares is higher than that of the large ones).* As they profit by this operation, they neither dislike the labor involved nor do they consider the unworthiness of the business and its dangers.

The unwise transferring of shares from the one group of speculators to the other (which is the only transferring that these shares undergo) enhances the noise, the shouting, and the bustle that prevails on the day of settlement. (On week-days the settlement is made in the Exchange [building]; on Sundays and holidays in the main street.) So great is the noise that some folk believe themselves to be attacked; others fear to be killed. He who has bought large shares and sold ducaton shares, makes efforts to have the stick kept low [i.e., the trading continued a few minutes] in order to reap the profit from the small shares, and to continue his engagements in the large shares. He, however, who has bought ducaton shares because he has sold large shares [short], demands the stick to be lifted up, in order to secure his profit, and will await the conclusion of his business with the large shares, hoping for yet a greater profit. . . .

---

*This divergence may have derived from the difference in the monthly settlement dates.

Thomas de Vega describes the behavior of a fool who asked the physicians to let him swim in a lake, but when he found that the water rose up to his throat, he regained his sound mind, recovered his health, and remained in that state. Oh, how many sick persons are there in the stock-gambling who resemble the fool, who throw themselves into this sea [of speculation] and who, when the waters reach their necks, return to firm ground. But the worst of all is that they are not aware of the remedy when bewildered they plunge into this whirlpool. Of the crocodile it is said that it is the biggest lizard that grows from the smallest beginning. From the little beginning of the ducaton shares there have developed the activities of the slyest speculators; and nobody feels uneasy about it nor feels that he need apologize for it. . . .

The speculators believe in vain that through abandoning the business in large shares they can avoid their irrevocable destiny and can free themselves from the fetters of the [gambling in] stocks. But they will discover that by engaging in the trading in ducaton shares, they just prolong the agony. . . . As I pointed out before, the speculators make innumerable transactions in order that [any particular] loss will not bear too heavily on them. . . . Although one can read our losses from our eyes, we get into the business deeper and deeper. May God keep us from losing everything!

The pleasure in this gamble has grown to such an extent that people who cannot gamble a ducaton per point risk a stuiver, and those to whom a stuiver is too much, risk a still smaller coin. Even children who hardly know the world and at best own a little pocket money agree that each point by which the large shares rise or fall will mean a certain amount of their pocket money for their small shares. . . . If one were to lead a stranger through the streets of Amsterdam and ask him where he was, he would answer, "Among speculators," for there is no corner [in the city] where one does not talk shares.

The two main reasons for the introduction of this kind of speculation [i.e., that in ducaton shares] was the greed of the brokers, and the need of the other people who invented the gamble. To make it quite clear, be it remarked that there are three reasons for the greediness of the brokers, and that on these accounts many have already been ruined. First, they want to earn the brokerage fees; secondly, they wish to make quick gains [on their own dealings] out of the price fluctuations; thirdly, they wish to live in comfort.

[1] If they try to achieve all these ends [at one time], they will easily meet with failure, for, when seeking to secure a large brokerage income, they have to offer or to take large batches of stock [on their own account]; and thus they may easily be caught (or in Dutch language "hanged"). Thus they are dependent [on a flow] of fresh news and are exposed to ruin.

[2] The brokers who intend to seek quick gains through price changes, i.e., by getting large orders from their customers and speculating extensively [on their own account] in executing these orders, experience the same fate. For, although it is not their intention to keep the shares [bought for their clients] for any length of time at their own risk, they cannot foresee incidents that may occur suddenly during this time [while they are holding the shares].

[3] He who devotes himself voluntarily to the business, in order to meet with intelligence and courage all its vicissitudes, will have the greater satisfaction, the stronger become the attacks, but in the end [even] he will have to confess that the business is such that he is always in the dark, that it is always risky, and that it is always frightening.

In order to gain from [the second] of the three methods mentioned above, the brokers must be popular at the stock exchange, for if, at the conclusion of the business, they are asked about their customers, they need the help of a good friend who will sign the contracts for them and will conceal the true character of the affair. This concealment and cloaking of the orders has spread in such a manner that even the merchants make use of the manoeuvre, although this also may prove detrimental to guileless people.

When the merchants come to know about an event which certainly will bring about a change of the price, they turn to the brokers in order to derive benefit from this change. But they give their orders only to those who will not

JOSEPH DE LA VEGA

divulge their names before the order is carried out, for it seems to them that the financial standing of the principal [giving the order] might be doubted [or] that the price might be changed before its execution. . . .

If a broker receives an order of this character,* he does not dare conclude the transaction lest people take notice of the order and [later] blame him for executing the deal. He is afraid of a [possible] reaction on the price or of attracting unfavorable attention. He is suspicious that by means of further inquiries one may discover who his customer is and [then] that nobody would sell the shares to him on his own account. Consequently, his selfish interest struggles with his faithfulness, his ambition with his fears, profit with conscience, until in the end the broker decides to discuss the matter with a friend, who in his own name sells so many thousand pounds of ducaton shares and thus enables him to remain behind the scenes.

Although brokers were the original inventors of this gamble, people less favorably situated entered it. To be sure, the greater part of the profits from this gambling are spent on cards, dice, wine, banquets, gifts, ladies, carriages, splendid clothing, and other luxuries. Nevertheless there are also numerous people in the business simply for the reason of providing decently for their families. . . .

Some gamble for the fun of it, some for vanity, many are spendthrifts, many find satisfaction in their occupation, and quite a few [just] make a living here [at the stock exchange]. If they are hit by bad luck and are unable to prevent their own downfall, they at least try to save their honor. They take premiums, refund the invested money, pay the differences, the furore subsides, their troubles ease, the confusion is overcome, and the attack defeated.

This [namely, the possibility of avoiding a complete catastrophe] is the reason why so many jump into this whirlpool.

---

*De la Vega here anticipates what he explains at some length shortly, i.e., that this broker is affiliated with the party of the bulls. He also takes here the special case of an event which will have a depressing effect on the price of the stock.

And it is easier to count those who do not deal with ducaton shares than those who do.

Fourth Dialogue

Shareholder: In the first dialogue I dealt with the beginnings and the etymology of the stock exchange, with the wealth of the Company, . . . the considerable extension of the speculation, and the meaning of the premium business, while I made some allusion to the swindling manoeuvres.

In the second dialogue I explained to you the instability of prices and the reasons therefor, gave advice for a successful speculation, pointed out the causes of the ups and downs, talked about the fears of the bears and courageous attitude of the bulls, about the results of the bold enterprise of the latter and the significance of the timid procedure of the former, about the signs of the upheavals and their incomprehensibility, the frenzy and the foolishness of the speculation, the language used on the exchange, and the expressions which are customary there.

In the third dialogue I began to explain to you various transactions, to teach you some of the rules [of the game], and to clarify some of the business practices. I talked about the equity of the contracts, the time of delivery, the place of the transference of the shares, the location of the business, the indecent behavior [on the Exchange], the unrest, the vulgarities, the handshakes, the impossibility of getting out of the Exchange frenzy, the West Indian Company, the principles of the ducaton speculation, the types of Exchange people, the delay in the settlement of the accounts, the varieties of brokers, their conscientiousness, their risks, and their temerity. Therefore, only a description of the most speculative part of the business is now left to me, the climax of the Exchange transactions, the acme of Exchange operations, the craftiest and most complicated machinations which exist in the maze of the Exchange and which require the greatest possible cunning. . . .

Some ten or twelve persons [will, for example,] get together at the Exchange and form a ring (which is called a "Cabala," as already mentioned). When this ring thinks it advisable to sell shares, the means for prudently carrying out this purpose are given much thought. The members initiate action only when they can foresee its result, so that, apart from unlucky incidents, they can reckon on a rather sure success. . . .

They [the ring of the bears] strike the first blow with time sales, reserving the cash sales for the moment of greater distress. They sell 50,000 pounds for various [forward] months, an operation through which a decline of prices is bound to occur. The declining tendency spreads, the [ring of the] bears receives help from other speculators, and it becomes obvious that, with so broad a participation, the object [of the machinations] is sure to be achieved. The leaders of such manoeuvres can be called "Princes of the Tail," as Amadeo I of Savoy was called the "Duke of the Tail" because of his numerous suite. This expression can be applied to the leaders of the bears because of the untold hosts of adherents, or because their followers *cling* to them, or because these followers should carry their leaders' trains. As there are so many people who cannot wait to follow the prevailing trend of opinion, I am not surprised that a small group becomes an army. [Most people] think only of doing what the others do and of following their examples. . . .

The first trick [of the bears' ring] is the following: in order to prevent numerous extensions of the contracts by which the great financiers buy shares for cash and sell them on term, contenting themselves with [a spread in price equivalent to] the interest on the money invested, the ring arranges sales for later dates at the same price at which the shares are being sold for cash; in the hope of a greater profit, they do not pay attention to the loss of interest. They are like Aesop's dog which let go the meat because its shadow appeared bigger to him.

Secondly, a broker in whom the syndicate has confidence is given the order to buy secretly a batch of shares from an [avowed] bull, without revealing his real principal. But he sells the very same shares with a good deal of publicity, while it is shouted out that even the bulls are making sales. As the broker wants to sell to one bull the same shares he has bought from another bull, the first one sees that the story about the sales of the latter is true. Alarmed, the second bull sells his shares also. Seized by fear, everybody tries to forestall the sales of the others and regards any advice to buy as deceitful. Such a panic we call "to be in tortures,"* and innumerable [traders] take to their heels . . . when even the slightest suspicion is roused. . . .

Thirdly, the syndicate of the bears sells some blocks of shares for cash to one of the wealthy people who live on the hypothecation of stocks. As it is known that the latter [as a matter of course] sell at once for future delivery the shares which they have bought for cash, the syndicate bids its broker [charged with the execution of the manoeuvre], before the fixing of the prices [of the day], to send a message very secretly to the agent of every business firm [represented on the Exchange], a communication which will soon be an *open secret,* to the effect that the great capitalist has received important news, and that alarmed by it he intends to sell stocks. When afterwards the sales are actually made, the swindle seems to be verified, the aim is reached, fear spreads, and a crash of prices is brought about. But the panic can easily be explained if the speculators suspect a change of opinion by their protectors and see their foundations shaken.

Fourthly, at the beginning of a campaign, the syndicate borrows all the money available at the Exchange and makes it apparent that it wishes to buy shares with this money. Afterwards, however, large *sales* are executed. Thus two birds are killed with one stone. First, the Exchange is supposed to believe that the original plan is altered because of important news; secondly, the bulls are prevented from finding money for hypothecating their shares. They are, therefore, compelled to sell, since they do not have the money to take up the stock [or else fall into the trap described as the seventh stratagem]. . . .

The fifth stratagem [of the syndicate] consists in selling the largest possible quantity of call options in order [apparently by the absorption of available loan funds] to bring pressure on

---

*In the original, the Spanish phrase is *tener calcetas.*

the payers of premiums to sell the stocks if they exercise their right to call.

The sixth stratagem is to enter into as many put contracts as possible, until the receivers of the premiums [assumed to be bulls] do not dare to buy more stock [on their own initiative]. [Their hands will be largely tied] because they are already obliged to take the stock [covered by the put premiums, if requested so to do]. Therefore the speculation for a decline has free course and is an almost sure success. We say of those who buy by means of a forward call contract and sell at a fixed [future] term or of those who sell by means of a put contract and buy at a fixed [future] term *that they shift the course of their speculation.* But as [the course chosen] may turn out to be the wrong [line of] speculation and the right way can thus be missed, [such a shift] is rarely made.

The seventh stratagem is to recognize that the bulls are in need of shares to survive the siege; and so [the bears] give them money. Then [the bears] sell the hypothecated shares again and, with the difference between what they receive on the sales and what they loan on the shares, they are able to engage in further call and put operations.*

This is a devilish trick, since, as it were, immortality is promised and death is given. It seems as if the bears give life to the bulls by lending them money [when they hypothecate] the stocks which the latter have bought; [but the ring turns around and sells these shares, so that the bulls have] to buy again the stocks which they had hypothecated. . . .

Although the bears lack shares, they do not blush to create the appearance of an abundance. The shares change hands, often fifty times in one week, rising and falling like balls [in a game], but this changing of hands is indicative only of the ruin of the business in shares. . . . What meaning does it have that

---

*The above rendering follows the Spanish original. However, the German translator believes that de la Vega made here a double mistake: he should have written "money" instead of "shares" in the first sentence, and he should have seen that the reference to put and call operations introduces an unnecessary, somewhat irrelevant idea.

the bears buy one share, when, protected by their alliance, they sell ten shares? What does it mean when they take over the hypothecated shares in order to pass them out again immediately? How can one suppress anxiety [about this situation] and how can one avoid lamentations? . . . Would scholars consider incorrect [a statement to the effect] that I cannot regard the purchase of one share a [*bona fide*] purchase when four are sold simultaneously, that I cannot consider a [*bona fide*] taking-up of one share [any transaction which entails that] ten shares be delivered simultaneously? . . .

The eighth trick [of the syndicate of the bears] is the following: if it is of importance to spread a piece of news which has been invented by the speculators themselves, they have a letter written and [arrange to have] the letter dropped as if by chance at the right spot. The finder believes himself to possess a treasure, whereas he has really received a letter of Uriah which will lead him into ruin. On his own initiative, he makes known the contents of the letter to his coterie and points out the reasons which will move the syndicate to sell when it receives news of this kind. And if a storm breaks out on the Exchange that very day, the news seems thus to be confirmed, the suspicion ratified, and the apprehensions explained. . . .

Ninthly, the syndicate encourages a friend whose judgment is esteemed, whose connections are respected, and who has never dealt in shares, to sell one or two lots of stock while the risk of loss is borne by the group. The notion [lying behind this manoeuvre] is the belief that anything new attracts attention, and that therefore the decision of this person [to sell stocks] will produce astonishment and will have important consequences. . . .

The tenth trick [of the syndicate] is to whisper into the ear of an intimate friend (but loud enough to be heard by those who lie in wait for it) that he should sell if he wants to make money. . . . "The stones speak," says the prophet, and "the walls have ears," says the proverb; and our conspirators know this truth to be verified by experience. If their secret spreads, their advice [seems to have met] with approval, and

[when] it becomes obvious that they sell blocks of stock, the walls and the stones do [appear] to talk; people seek the secret reasons of the [whispered] assertions; one is grateful for the hint; and, as cheating a close friend is thought impossible, the manoeuvre meets with success, the fish take the bait, the net becomes filled, the victory is celebrated, and the intention of the ring is very advantageously achieved.

Eleventhly, the Contremine [i.e., the syndicate] carries out the following trick in order to reach its aim: they are not content to wound their enemies with their tongue, which Jeremiah compares to an arrow, and to fight them with their teeth . . . and with arguments. In order to insinuate that their own concern is founded on grave considerations and does not refer exclusively to the situation of the Company, the bears sell government obligations. Thus the bulls are to be made to believe that discord is dominating the state and that there is a reason to be alarmed about and to pay attention to a possible outbreak of war. . . . This recourse to selling long and short-term state obligations may seem to be of but small importance for the business [in stocks], but whoever thinks so is in error. . . . Our speculators [i.e., the bulls] are paralyzed in their stock dealings, and are bled by their engagements [to protect the market] in state bonds, [all because of a trumped-up allegation of a] situation perilous to the country, dangers threatening the Company, and a breakdown of the share market.

Finally, the ring practices a twelfth manoeuvre. In order to be well-informed about the tendency of the market, even the bears [before launching their big operation] begin with purchases and take all items [offered]. If the shares rise in price, they pocket the quick profit; if the prices fall, however, they sell at a loss, content to have ascertained the weakening tendency. Moreover, the interest which the timid public takes in their proceedings is already useful to them, since the public thinks that conditions must be serious when the speculators sell at a loss. This is one of the most powerful available stratagems for influencing the wavering elements. If [the timid souls] see the bears buy, they do not know whether the latter buy in order to sell later (which in the Exchange language means to "look for powder"), or whether they buy because they have changed their opinion or given up their position and therefore really want to buy. If the Contremine decides upon this dissimulation, they offer for the stocks more than the price of the day (what we call "inflating" the price). They influence the price in this way in order to sell [short] at the higher figure and thus to gain in the end. God with one breath breathed life into Adam, whereas the bears take the life of many people by inflating the price [of the shares]. . . .

Merchant: Do the poor bulls have no means [of defense] against these manoeuvres?

Shareholder: They certainly have. There is protection against the most daring attacks, and even the greatest slyness finds its master. Inasmuch, however, as the means employed in the pursuit of either of these objectives is the same—really those already traced out in the case of the bears—I fear that the two-sided manoeuvres stand in the same position [as that just described, i.e., subject to moral condemnation]. Therefore in order to avoid prolixity and repetition, I shall pass over in silence the measures taken by the bulls; [instead] I shall tell you only of the practices of a few sly brokers, who, were they not unscrupulous, would find themselves applauded.*

A broker, for example, receives an order to sell 20 shares; if a broker for the bulls receives the order, he begins to perspire from fear and to rage with fury, for, if he sells first the shares bought on his own account, he fears that it will become known and that he will be accused [of sharp practice]. If he keeps his own shares and carries out the sale as ordered, he fears a slump in consequence of the sales so that he could dispose of his own shares only at a great loss. Finally he decides to be honest . . . and from mere fear [of discovery] tries to give up his own interests in order to be able to serve better the order entrusted to him. [But] people scent this [kind of] dissimulation; the Contremine is again encouraged; a shouting begins, "There are pirates near the coast"; another shouts, "Such and

---

*In this section, de la Vega has reference to the so-called "free" brokers, who participate in the speculation on their own accounts.

such a person must have taken a purgative. He sells as much as he can for secret clients"; a third says, "He is troubled with diarrhoea"; another jests, "He lays eggs"; and all unanimously declare, "He is poisoning the Exchange." These are the expressions which our speculators use in such incidents and which are customary on these occasions. All this does not impress the taciturn broker, for, as he carries out his order to the best of his ability, he will [merely] consider it annoying that the order became known before its execution. But this is a pain which does not go very deeply. As it does not pierce his heart, he feels like a benefactor who causes no losses. . . .

The broker in question was doing business on his own account because he expected a rich profit. If [in such a situation] he gets an order, the carrying-out of which binds him in a direction contrary to his own transactions, his heart trembles, his appearance changes, his language becomes heated, his throat goes tight, the voice becomes frightened, the breath stops, and unless he is . . . skillful in escaping from danger . . . , he perishes wretchedly and dies as a fool. . . . In order to avoid this, our broker sells his own shares secretly. He tries to kill the snake around a man's neck without hurting the man; he seeks to avoid the damage [to his own interests] without acting harmfully as far as the specific order is concerned. It would be better to avoid these troubles and to save the pressures on one's heart [by trading only for clients]. What use is it to him to earn something (provided he earns anything at all) if, with the forfeiture of his reputation, he loses his brokerage business and, with the loss of the latter, he is deprived of his fortune? . . .

It is even more noteworthy if an unselfish broker endeavors to carry out a large order wisely and cleverly. For, if he tries to buy . . . , all his efforts are directed toward acquiring some shares quickly with the hope that by fortunate bargaining he may secure the rest afterwards [at a reasonable price]. In order to conceal his intentions, he sometimes offers a batch [of shares], and sometimes he asks for offers. If shares are then thrust at him, his purpose has met with success. If one tries to take shares from him, he has [in effect] already bought [the lot that he was charged to buy]; and, without affecting the price [on the Exchange] he obtains double the brokerage fee.* He thrusts his sword about with most admirable agility, and gives such a pleasing performance that one regrets that he is not always successful. . . .

Ingenuity and audacity [on the part of the broker] are able [at times] to achieve success even if the circumstances of the Exchange are unfavorable, a success which becomes thus all the more admirable.

Again, if a broker, who on his own account is already speculating for a decline, receives an order for a sale, well, there is nothing which equals the joyful mood of such a broker.

Our speculators frequent certain places which are called *coffy-huysen* or coffee-houses because a certain beverage is served there called *coffy* by the Dutch and *Caffé* by the Levantines. The well-heated rooms offer in winter a comfortable place to stay, and there is no lack of manifold entertainment. You will find books and board games, and you will meet there with visitors with whom you can discuss affairs. One person takes chocolate, the others coffee, milk, and tea; and nearly everybody smokes while conversing. None of this occasions very great expense; and while one learns the news, he negotiates and closes transactions.

When a bull enters such a coffee-house during the Exchange hours, he is asked the price of the shares by the people present. He adds one to two per cent to the price of the day and he produces a notebook in which he pretends to put down orders. The desire to buy shares increases; and this enhances also the apprehension that there may be a further rise (for on this point we are all alike: when the prices rise, we think that they fly up high and, when they have risen high, that they will run away from us). Therefore, purchase orders are given to the cunning broker. But, in order slyly to reach his own objectives,

---

* Presumably the broker is allowed to charge his principal for the spurious offer to sell, withdrawn at the instance of the principal, as well as for the purchase order that was really executed.

199

he replies that he has so many other orders that he cannot be at anyone else's disposal. The naïve questioner believes in the sincerity of the statement; his desire to buy becomes even more ardent; and he gives an unrestricted order to another broker. As soon as this becomes known to the sly [first] fellow, the latter hurries to the Exchange and offers the shares at more than the day's price. The other broker, previously uninterested, buys at the higher price because he believes there to be new reasons making for the change in the price and enhancing the desire for investment. At times the increase in the price is maintained, deception has been crowned with success, and what seemed originally as madness comes to have the appearance of cleverness. . . .

One of the neatest tricks which take place in these circles is for some of the bulls to pose as bears. This is done for two reasons. First, because the opponents [the real bears] imagine that, if they [are able to] buy a share from among those held back and concealed, the other party [that of the bulls] has changed its ideas and, instead of building silver bridges for them, seek to drag them down. . . . Now the bulls change the price so that they [the bears] are forced to pay dearly for the shares which they have sold short [in their attempt to subdue the bulls]. Thus the bulls reach their aim, and thus they defeat their malevolent enemies through pretence, and thus by cautious manoeuvres they deceive these opponents who are trying to deceive them.

Secondly, these speculators resort to such a trick in order, in sudden conjunctures, to sell without producing a panic. As it is taken for granted that these [particular] speculators undoubtedly belong to the Contremine, the bulls rally around furiously in order to buy the shares offered by the first group, on the assumption that they have to stand by their opinions and have to make sacrifices for them.

One man [a broker] tries to find out what is happening in an assemblage on the Exchange. Therefore he puts his head through the arms of the persons forming the group (quite unmindful of the unpleasant smells of perspiration), and learns that eight [588] is offered for the shares without anybody agreeing to that price. The broker then turns away, and joins the group from the other side, pretending to have heard nothing, and to have a purchase order without restriction as to price. He begins to bid eight and a half; his followers screw up courage and offer nine; and finally this brings success, causing exultation and winning applause. If an electric eel is placed among dead fish, the latter make movements again when pushed about by its contortions. The bulls [similarly] seem to be dead before they are awakened and revived by this broker through his voice, through his lies, and through his courage. Everything he undertakes is done in an energetic and mercurial fashion, and this lively and vivacious rogue can even effect a resurrection of the dead. When at the sight of the wolf the cattle become silent, and the frog takes on a pale color the moment it is looked at, how wonderful it is that even the bears become silent and grow pale on such an occasion? . . .

There are three [commonly used] formulas by which a purchase or sale of shares can be initiated. [A seller states], "I give them to you at this price"; or he says, "I give them at that price" without further explanation. Or you say, "I give them at this price to everybody who wants to have them." [In addition, there are formulas not commonly employed because they are so dangerous.] Whoever says [merely], "I give them," has no escape from delivering at any price on demand; and if this person, later regretting his bargain, is not liberated from his obligation out of friendship, there is nothing left for him to do except to pray, complain, and suffer. Whoever says, "I give them to anybody who wants them," exposes himself to a great danger, for there are people who count on such a broad offer, as if their daily bread depended on it. Since the status, the insignificant capital, the low reputation, and the limited trustworthiness of such people are well known, they do not dare attempt to carry on any considerable business. But if they hear of such a generous offer as that made by our braggart, they rapidly disconcert him by shouting. "They are mine!" Thus he is punished for his [excess of] confidence, and he lives to repent his rashness.

He who says merely, "I give," does so with an equivocal aim. . . . For his wish is not to sell but to cause the prices to move. If there is someone who expressed a desire to buy, [the dealer's] prompt answer is, "I give, but not to you," and, as he cannot be obligated to anything else because—strictly speaking—he had said only, "I give," he is always fighting with a two-edged sword and a double-barrelled pistol.

I am not surprised that there are brokers who (if their names are well enough known) countersign their contracts, "N.N. by order." They are tempted to act like this by an eagerness to deal on their own accounts, and they choose this kind of countersignature to suggest that the business is done only on "order" of a customer. Thus they understand how to cloak their avarice and to screen their foolishness.

I am more surprised that already for a long time some enterprising brokers have run [two establishments], one for true brokerage and another for Exchange transactions on their own accounts. At the delivery of the stocks they have designated themselves as principals, and promoted the idea that a change in the name meant an actual change. A man with his wife tried to pay in a public house for only one person by reference to the words of God that man and wife were of one flesh. But when the landlord realized that they utilized sophistry to his detriment, he made efforts to repay them in their own coin and demanded that the two should pay for eleven, for, if two were one, then the number one put twice side by side is eleven. It seems that the stratagem of the artful brokers is in conformity with the shrewdness of the landlord, for each of them tries to imagine that he can occupy five places, playing at the same time the role of broker, merchant, contractor, lawyer, and judge. . . .

It is with reason, however, that [any] faction of the Exchange is in dismay when the most influential and most respected of their brokers, under whose protection they have been standing, leave them. Such a broker serves (we can assume) the most select, wealthiest, and most enterprising people of the Exchange. The bulls are his customers; and the pursuit of his principals' best interests is ever the object of his even-handed zeal. One day an ingenious bear recognizes that the price of stocks is beginning to waver. In order to stimulate a more rapid fall of the price, he gives an [honest] broker an order to sell ten shares without revealing the name of his principal. The broker carries out the order honestly, cleverly, and discreetly because all he wants is to earn the brokerage fee, although he is obviously causing damage to his friends [the bulls]. His followers are amazed, and he is asked whether he is selling for patrons. They ask him whether he has any recent news. He gives no answer. They want to know whether he has to sell many shares. He is silent. Therefore his former followers, (furious about his change of heart and his treason), in order to cause him trouble and to prevent him from arranging a profitable sale, cause the prices to rise, accusing him of ingratitude in leaving their advantage out of consideration. When the truth is revealed which had been ingeniously concealed, the bear who gave the order has already attained his objective, he has sown disharmony, has caused the prices to change, and can boast of his complete success. . . .

Numerous [brokers] are inexhaustible in inventing [involved manoeuvres], but for just this reason do not achieve their purposes. The bulls spread a thousand rumors about the stocks, of which one would be enough to force up the prices. A thousand stratagems of the Contremine are launched in an effort to cause ill-temper on the exchange. If by chance, however, some of the fabrications come to be confirmed, the real situation may turn out to be of less consequence [than one might anticipate]. If it becomes known, for instance, that a situation is not as favorable as one feared, the prices rise in spite of a deterioration of the situation. On the other hand, a decline [of values may] set in when a propitious event falls short of expectations.

When a cunning broker [interested in a price rise] has to buy two thousand pounds [worth of shares], he first buys but one thousand pounds [worth] in order to convey the impression that he will take [stocks worth] at least twenty [thousand] pounds. As soon as he sees that another [broker] buys too, whether to follow his example or to flatter him, he approaches the latter and talks to him in a hushed voice expressing anguish (but audibly enough to be heard by those who make efforts to catch his remarks). He implores the other for Heaven's sake not to ruin him and not to influence the prices, for he has still to take care of a tremendous volume, and if there were a disturbance the transaction would be a failure, and a loss inevitable. Now the Exchange takes as a serious endeavor what is only a ruse. Immediately everyone begins to buy in order to secure the profit which, according to the [presumed] tendency, is to be expected. Though the success of this trick is not wholly certain, it is often worth trying. The evil spirit gave the advice to Eve to eat from the Forbidden Tree that she might become immortal. If this had been possible, the evil spirit would not have given his advice, for he gave advice only for his own advantage. It is just the same with the actions of the evil spirits on our Exchange. If, however, they try—as described above—to persuade their friends not to buy shares in order to buy them themselves and if, in asking the friends not to influence the prices, they [act in a manner] themselves that alters prices, such an artifice possesses something almost divine. . . .

When a generous broker wants to favor a relative, he [may have to] approach him a hundred times before he is able [actually] to give the necessary information without being overheard by those who lie in wait for [such presumably choice] data. From fear of this contingency . . . , abbreviated words are used, and from this expediency misunderstandings ensue, because often the opposite of what was intended is understood. One day I asked a gentleman who was busily engaged on his own affairs what in his opinion was likely to happen. He answered excitedly, "Ven."* I thought he called me; I followed him, and saw that he bought many shares at a public house without telling me anything else. So I assumed that "Ven" meant that I should follow him, and the purchases signified that I should also buy. Highly satisfied with the suggestions, I hurried to the Exchange, and bought there a small batch of shares, when I suddenly noticed that my adviser sold eight shares in one lot. Offended [at

---

* *Ven* is a conspicuous element in the Spanish words *venir* and *vender,* meaning "come" and "sell."

this apparent perfidy], I complained that he had invited me to join his operation and that he had deceived me in a very offensive manner. But he assured me (actually confirming this assertion by further sales) that he had used the shares acquired secretly merely to shake the position of his enemies. He said that he had also advised me sufficiently that I should sell by telling me repeatedly, "Ven," and that he could not have uttered it more distinctly lest someone should have heard it. . . .

Despicable meanness is the appropriate characterization of the practice of [a few] brokers who (concealing their real intentions under the appearance of complaisance) act in the following manner even though they are thought dishonorable for doing so, namely, they advise an intimate friend to sell, despite the fact that they have a purchase order. Even worse, they cause the sale of shares which they themselves through somebody else have pressed on the person concerned, as if it were not very easy to deceive an unsuspecting person. . . .

Merchant: We ask you to reward our attention only by telling us the reason of the [recent] unheard-of collapse in the price of the shares, which spelled such a deplorable crash in so short a time.

Shareholder: Yes, I shall do so with great pleasure. That you may listen more calmly I will mention that the price has risen again to 465 from the 365 to which the shares had fallen, and is holding at this level. But be aware of the many traps which the evil spirit has laid in the path of the bulls. . . . In the book of Job, the evil spirit says to God that he has roamed over the earth. I believe that before our misfortune [this same evil spirit] visited the sea and the land, since unfavorable news arrived from both hither and yon and constituted the starting point of the fatal events. On land there was peace and calm everywhere; on the Exchange, a goodly supply of money and abundant credit were available; there were splendid prospects for exports; a vigorous spirit of enterprise [manifested itself]; brilliant military forces under famous leaders were [protecting the country]; there was favorable news, incomparable knowledge of business, a swelling population, a strong fleet, advantageous alliances. Therefore not the slightest concern, not the least apprehension reigned, not the smallest cloud, not the most fleeting shadow was to be seen.

By sea a letter arrived from the governor of the Cape of Good Hope (which was delivered by French ships). The letter contained the news that in India things were going on as everyone would wish and that the ships from India had arrived [at the Cape] with the richest of cargoes. These fortunate circumstances were explained partly by the opening of the Chinese market and partly by the discovery of new mines. At any rate, everyone anticipated good harvests and a favorable economic situation. In wide circles a miracle was expected, so great as to surprise everybody.

Only one circumstance ran counter to these promising prospects. This was the news that one of the most heavily laden ships had returned from the Cape to Batavia because she had not been able to continue her voyage by reason of a dangerous list. But even this annoyance was lightly regarded since it was assumed that this ship would sail with the *Naa Schepen,* that is, two or three smaller ships departing from Batavia some months after the first which generally brought cargoes to the value of four tons [of gold] as well as the books, accounts, and balance sheets of the East Indian administration for the use of the directors [in the Netherlands]. A few days before the arrival of the first squadron, [a different but] apparently quite reliable report was spread that this squadron had run aground on a sandbank but was out of danger; and further that the ship that had turned back had actually sailed in the convoy of the fleet. Such news, agreeable to the bulls and important as far as dividends were concerned, aroused the spirit of Ahab and Satan [on the Exchange]. Everybody who did not join in the jubilation was regarded as a fool, and everyone who sold shares was looked at as a tenacious and deadly enemy of his own interests, each sale being called foolishness, madness, and a crime.

The ships arrived safely in the harbor, and the directors read part of the incoming letters. When it was rumored that the freight (of the goods purchased [in India] called *Inkoop*) amounted to the value of only 34 tons [of gold] compared with 50 tons last year, the mood changed and optimism ceased. But the blow could not have been so severe if the Contremine had not speculated on a rise too. Baffled by the magnificent prospects, they had not dared to wage a battle. Had the Contremine sold [short] a goodly number of shares, it would have had sufficient advantage, when prices fell 20 per cent in the first movement, [to have bought stock to cover its commitments], and would have pocketed the profit. The collapse of prices [in the whole crash] would not have been so violent. But, as some people wanted to sell in order not to lose still more [than they already stood to lose], others to avoid any loss at all, others again in order still to gain something, the selling became general, and dejection supervened everywhere. Those who were compelled to take delivery [of shares contracted for earlier], sold again in order to be able to cover their obligations. He who was in the possession of hypothecated shares sold them because their value had sunk under the amount of the sum borrowed [to carry them]. He who had bought sold lest he should lose even more, and sold still more in order to make up for the [earlier] loss. The few sellers who had already sold short [purposefully] caused a further fall of the prices, encouraged by the prospect of a profit and seeking to exploit their luck. In the end people went begging with the shares [as it were], as if one asked alms of the [prospective] purchaser. Such a panic, such an inexplicable shock was produced that the whole world seemed to crumble, the earth to be submerged, and the heavens to fall.

The general atmosphere began to improve when the contents of a second series of Company letters were made known. It appeared that by the sale of the 34 tons [of this year's import] just as much could be gained [because of the higher prices] as from the 50 tons of the year before. So the bears crowded together and, in order not to let the bulls take breath, spread the rumor that a war would break out. [They said that] they knew of so many secret preparatory measures that no doubt could be entertained. Then the taxes would increase like an avalanche, the burdens would grow immeasurably, the whole of Europe would be set ablaze, and misery, terror, and ruin would be found everywhere. Even those were alarmed who already had a notion of the scheme projected by the Contremine. [Consequently], the bears were able exclusively to control the market prices. To such an extent were they the masters of the situation that they refrained from selling shares against cash, merely to avoid a suspension of payments, wishing to have a few solvent people left. Thus the stock exchange came into the sad plight that I have just described; and even a few persons who were regarded as quite substantial sought the shelter provided for over-extended purchasers of options [they appealed to the decree of Frederick Henry]. Here the wise saying is confirmed that like Saul you often seek David in his bed and find only a statue. On the Exchange, too, one found stones instead of men, and its strongest supporters collapsed like thin sticks.

In the ducaton speculation the damage was still more disturbing. (Speculation [in these imaginary units] was declared by court decisions to be a game or a bet, and thus the transactions in them were denied the character of true business.) Therefore it was not even necessary to appeal to Frederick Henry's decree in order to refuse payment.

When, in this pocket-picking, each 500 pounds [worth of stock, equal to 3,000 gulden] was diminished 300 gulden and afterwards 500 gulden, the speculators behaved in quite variant ways. A few men of honor paid everything, and others at least a part, as far as their fortunes went. But there were also persons who, under the influence of the sudden suspension of business (of which no one spoke any more), paid nothing, but they demanded nothing either. One group of brokers did not pay because of complete insolvency; again others had to refuse payments as their business connections became weak and their resources did not suffice. There were even people who boasted of their suspension of payments and who possessed the objectionable brazenness to say that they made money out of dirt in order to cheat their creditors. If these men had been polite instead of impudent, they would have said at least that man is made of dust, and, as they could do nothing else for the satisfaction of their creditors, they gave what they were themselves, namely, dust, and thus would offer their bodies instead of other sacrifices. . . .

[As things turned out], the importations [of the East India Company] yielded an exceedingly fine result. But here . . . the light was hidden as in a jug [as was true of Gideon's army]. Only the quantities imported, but not their values, were known. The bold speculators (as I told you) did not see the splendor of the transactions but only the *cover* which hid the latter. After the examination of the latest business letters [from India], it turned out that the sale of the cargoes was to yield excellent revenues. The vessel broke, and the light became visible, but at the same moment the bears sounded the trumpet, and shouted that war would be declared.

What a terrible cruelty it was that these destroyers of the Exchange made pass for an accomplished fact not only what was going to happen, but even things that could only *possibly* occur! The bears foresaw that [under certain circumstances] the United Provinces would wage war, and this presumption was a sufficient basis for them to proclaim the outbreak of the war. Yet I am not surprised at [their forecast], but at the fact that, in the mere possibility of the war, they saw the outbreak already certain. . . .

This, my friends, is all that I have to say about the [late] misfortunes on the stock exchange, although my presentation gives only a pale picture of the events. . . .

Everyone was involved in the speculation. When it began, the Exchange presented a rosy picture; when it ended, a sad one. . . . The watchword *Audaces fortuna juvat* . . . has no validity relative to the [East India] Company for we see that from trading in its shares the audacious did not win but were prostrated.

In spite of these difficulties, [however] I advise you to speculate for a rise and not for a fall. The sincerity of my words is confirmed by the circumstance that I recommend something that has caused me losses, and that I think good something that has ruined me. I advise you well just because of my misfortune. . . . And, that you may see that a revival of the stock exchange has already been brought about, I draw your attention to the fact that the shares which had gone down by 180 per cent because of the apprehension of an outbreak of the war have risen again by 100 per cent [of the face value] since its declaration. . . .

What makes me especially sad is the sudden end of the ducaton speculation, on which so many decent people and so many men with small means subsisted. For this tree had sunk so many roots that nobody thought the trunk likely to fall in the first storm, and the high prices suddenly to decline. . . . Sad indeed is a catastrophe that annihilates at one stroke names, dreams, persons, fortunes, and reputations.

Julius Caesar made use of aid from the mathematician Sosigenes to alter the inconstant lunar year into the constant astronomical year of 365 days 6 hours, and to fix the equinox on always the same day. As it was necessary to alter the dates of all festive days . . . and to put in two intercalary months, the year of transition was ordinarily called the *Year of Confusion.* The ducaton speculators realized that on the first of September the liquidation of their transactions had to be completed. They, too, desired an astronomer to change the seasons and wished that the September [settlement] be prolonged until November in order to see whether a recovery of prices would occur and whether their anxiety could be ended. But though they did not secure that aim, the same effect was reached as with the alteration of the calendar. This year too was a *year of confusion* for many unlucky speculators declared in one voice that the present crisis was the labyrinth of labyrinths, the terror of terrors, the *confusion of confusions.* . . .

I suspend this discourse because agonies disturb my spirit. I request you to accept, as an indication of my friendship, the affection with which I have described to you the progress of this famous Company which, after certain ships had initiated voyages in 1594, was founded in 1602 (as I pointed out to you) by order of the States General, and which, despite the extensive oppositions of the Portuguese and the

Spaniards, could enjoy (such as it does enjoy) the conquest of so many kingdoms and the tribute of so many kings. . . .

On geographical maps fine dotted lines are drawn around undiscovered regions which are named *Terra incognita.* On the Exchange, too, there are many secret operations which I have not been able to discover, but I make use of the trick of the geographers; until new investigations shall grant you knowledge, I have pointed out the objects to you by means of thin lines. I hope that as friends you will excuse the shortcomings of the presentation and as educated men compensate for my errors.

Merchant: I on my part thank you for the instruction. I esteem business but hate gambling. I have a notion that my faculties do not suffice for such complicated transactions. If I nearly lost my sense when I wanted to learn about the speculations, you may conclude of what importance to me is the conduct of Exchange transactions. It is possible that I shall become a holder of shares and shall deal [in shares] in an honest way, but I am very sure that I shall never become a speculator. . . .

Philosopher: I will take the same course because I am too old to defy dangers and to endure storms. I shall keep my shares until it shall please God that [after the recent downfall of the prices] I can get out of them in peace, for I will only save myself and not gather wealth. . . . All schools of philosophy teach that the soul is nobler than the body, life nobler than death, and the existent nobler than the non-existent. But, as for the stock exchange, I approve the paradoxical opinion of the Platonic musician that the non-existent is better than the existent. I think it much better not to be a speculator, [and in making that statement] I have in mind real speculation, not the honest business in shares, for what is fair in the latter is dubious in the former. . . .

SOURCES USED IN
INTRODUCTION TO
CONFUSIÓN DE CONFUSIONES

AMZALAK, MOSES BENSABAT, *Joseph de la Vega e o Seu Livro "Confusión de Confusiones"* (Lisbon, 1925), 16 pp.
Includes a list of Vega's writings.

———— *As Operações de Bôlsa Segundo Iosseph de la Vega ou José da Veiga Economista Portugués do Século XVII* (Lisbon, 1926), 32 pp.

———— "Joseph da Veiga and Stock Exchange Operations in the Seventeenth Century" (In Essays in Honour of the Very Rev. Dr. J. H. Hertz [London, 1944], pp. 33-49).

BARBOUR, VIOLET, *Capitalism in Amsterdam in the Seventeenth Century* (Baltimore, 1950), 171 pp. (The Johns Hopkins University Studies in Historical and Political Science, ser. 67, no. I).

BLOOM, HERBERT IVAN, *The Economic Activities of the Jews of Amsterdam in the Seventeenth and Eighteenth Centuries* (Williamsport, Pa., 1937), 332 pp.

COLE, ARTHUR HARRISON, *The Great Mirror of Folly (Het Groote Tafereel der Dwaasheid)* (Boston, 1949), 40 pp. (The Kress Library of Business and Economics, Publication no. 6).

DILLEN, JOHANNES GERARD VAN, "Isaac le Maire et le Commerce des Actions de la Compagnie des Indes Orientales", *Revue d'Histoire Moderne,* X (1935), pp. 121-137.

———— "Termijnhandel te Amsterdam in de 16de en 17re Eeuw", *De Economist,* LXXVI (1927), pp. 503-523.

EHRENBERG, RICHARD, "Die Amsterdamer Aktienspekulation im 17. Jahrhundert", *Jahrbücher für Nationalökonomie und Statistik,* 3rd ser., vol. 3 (1892), pp. 809-826.

Jongh, J. de, *De Nederlandsche Makelaardij . . . met een Voor Woord van P. A. Diepenhorst* (Haarlem, 1949), 262 pp.

Kellenbenz, Hermann, *Unternehmerkräfte im Hamburger Portugal- und Spanienhandel, 1590-1625* (Hamburg, 1954), 424 pp.

Laspeyres, Etienne, *Geschichte der Volkswirtschaftlichen Anschauungen der Niederländer und ihrer Literatur zur Zeit der Republik* (Leipzig, 1863), 334 pp. (Fürstlich Jablonowski'schen Gesellschaft zu Leipzig, XI).

Samuel, Ludwig, *Die Effektenspekulation im 17. und 18. Jahrhundert* (Berlin, 1924), 192 pp. (Betriebs- und Finanzwirtschaftlich Forschungen, II. serie, heft 13).

Sayous, André Emile, "La Bourse d'Amsterdam au XVIIᵉ Siècle", *Revue de Paris,* 1900, vol. 3, pp. 772-784.

——— "Die Grossen Händler und Kapitalisten in Amsterdam gegen Ende des Sechzehnten und Während des Siebzehnten Jahrnhunderts", *Weltwirtschaftliches Archiv,* 46.bd., heft 3 (1937), pp. 685-711; 47.bd., heft I (1938), pp. 115-144.

——— "La Spéculation sur Marchandises dans les Provinces-Unies au XVIIᵉ Siècle", *Bijdragen voor Vaderlandsche Geschiedenis en Oudheidkunde,* vol. IV, 3 (1903), pp. 24-36.

Smith, Marius Franciscus Johannes, *Tijd-Affaires in Effecten aan de Amsterdamsche Beurs* (The Hague, 1919), 234 pp.

Vaz Diaz, A. M., "Over den Vermogens Toestand der Amsterdamsche Joden in de 17ᵉ en de 18ᵉ Eeuw", *Tijdschrift voor Geschiedenis,* vol. 51 (1936), pp. 165-176.

Vega, Josseph De La, *Confusion de Confusiones . . . herdruk van den Spaanschen Tekt met Nederlandsche Vertaling, inleiding en toelichtingen door Dr. M. F. J. Smith; vertaling door Dr. G. J. Geers* (The Hague, 1939), 297 pp. (Nederlandsch *Economisch-Historisch Archief.* Werken, 10).

——— *Die Verwirrung der Verwirrungen; Vier Dialoge über die Börse in Amsterdam. Nach dem Spanischen original . . . übersetzt und eingeleitet von Dr. Otto Pringsheim* (Breslau, 1919), 233 pp.

Vergouwen, J. P., *De Geschiedenis der Makelaardij in Assurantiën hier te Lande tot 1813* (The Hague, 1945), 155 pp.